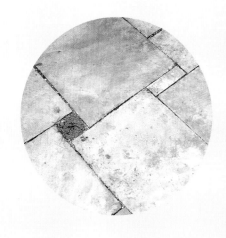

The Garden Floor

The Garden Floor

Nigel Colborn

New Holland

Published in 2000 by
New Holland Publishers (UK) Ltd
London • Cape Town • Sydney • Auckland

24 Nutford Place
London W1H 6DQ
United Kingdom

80 McKenzie Street
Cape Town 8001
South Africa

Level 1, Unit 4, 14 Aquatic Drive
Frenchs Forest, NSW 2086
Australia

Unit 1A, 218 Lake Road
Northcote, Auckland
New Zealand

Conceived, created and produced by
FOCUS PUBLISHING
The Courtyard
26 London Road
Sevenoaks
Kent TN13 1AP

ISBN 1 85974 274 2

Publishing Director Guy Croton
Art Director Glen Wilkins
Managing Editor Caroline Watson
Designer Sam Hemphill
Illustrator Ian Sidaway

2 4 6 8 10 9 7 5 3 1

Reproduction by Colour Symphony, Singapore
Printed and bound in Singapore by
Craft Print (Pte) Ltd

Contents

The Floor of Your Garden

In most gardens, the 'floor' is the centrepiece and most obvious feature of all. It can be made beautiful – even stunning – yet so often it is neglected.

How easy it is to take the most crucial part of your garden's design for granted! Whether planning a brand new garden from scratch, or restructuring an existing one, the tendency is to become preoccupied with how to fit everything in. And with garden sizes so often being smaller than one would like, fitting everything in is almost always a struggle. One builds up a wish list of desirable features – borders, seating area, pond, greenhouse, trees and shrubs, screens, hedges and so on – and then one wrestles with the dimensions of the site, eventually coming up with an arrangement that will meet as many needs as possible. The most crucial aspect of any garden's design, however, is not where these various constituents end up, but rather, what is done with the space between them.

Call it what you like – 'garden floor' is as useful a term as any – but the most used area of your garden is the ground space which separates the rest of the features. And the purpose of this book is to approach the whole concept of garden design – including planting – not in terms of the prominent features likely to be foremost in the minds of most designers, but rather, in terms of the horizontal spaces that connect them. After all, the impact of a fine building, a large structure – or even an outstanding natural feature – depends on rather more than its size and appearance. Where it sits, and how it relates to its surroundings often matters as much, if not more, than the building itself. How that subordinate space is furnished also matters a great deal, whether it is surfaced to make a sympathetic environment for the building, whether it is decorated to distract from it, or whether it is deliberately kept bland so as not to get in the way.

In a garden, ground surfaces can frequently play a far more dominant role than the more obvious structures. Whatever material is used to furnish a garden floor, it tends to create its own special effects – from the soft, cool greenness of, say, a lawn, to the hard, uncompromising surfaces of stone or concrete paving. With interiors, the choice of flooring is more or less limited to carpeting or some kind of cover; perhaps stone or timber – be it blocks or boards – or tiles. Outdoors, the range of possibilities is far wider. With grass alone, one can create a number of different surfaces: smooth, weed-free lawns, wildflower meadows, combinations of grass and other lawn plants or, as is used in most cases, durable areas of close-grown sward, disciplined once a week by mowing and capable of taking all the wear and tear of family life.

You can take things further, though, even with something as simple as grass. It is possible to develop an entire design structure by combining close-mown stretches with rougher areas. A long vista, for example, might have a neat, close-mown strip down its centre, leading your eye directly to some object at the far end, or to a distant view. But on either side of this strip, grass might be left to grow far longer, so that the midsummer effect is of waving stems and a gorgeous variety of grass flowers. There might be wildflowers, included among the grasses to attract butterflies and other insects, thus adding an extra dimension to the vista. And as the season advances, the resulting hay could be cut shorter, altering the appearance of the vista completely, and changing the rough-grass habitat so that, now, lower growing flowers – cyclamen, perhaps, or colchicums – can stud the cropped turf for an autumn display.

Stone or paving, incorporated into your main garden thoroughfares, could fulfil important aesthetic as well as practical needs. Popular routes around the garden will be subject to wear and tear, so it makes sense to floor them with durable materials. But there is more to hard landscaping than this. Such pathways link the main features or areas of interest in the garden but, as well as that, they can become design features which lead your eyes in the desired direction, punctuating the spaces between the various parts of the garden and giving relief from the monotony of a single surface. And they can, in themselves, become decorated or embellished so that they provide extra interest, whether at close quarters when walked along, or viewed from a distance.

RIGHT *A classic, beautifully mown green sward, enhanced by the brick terrace in the foreground and the ornamental trees along its borders. But there is so much more that can be done with grass in the garden.*

Carefully selected – and even more carefully placed – plants can enhance pathways, for example, sometimes with a diverting shape or bright colour, often formally arranged as punctuating points along the way, or perhaps simply with their fragrance.

As well as linking different parts of the garden, areas of garden floor can, of themselves, become important features or focal points. The cobbled design on page 41 is but one example of how easy it is to transform a small area of neutral interest into a centre point. The seating area at top right in the picture has been further enhanced, rather than being diluted by the design of the garden floor in that spot, making sitting there more pleasurable because the surroundings are more pleasing to look at.

In short, the floor space in your garden holds the key to better design for the *entire* garden, and should never be under-utilized and exploited.

The object of this book is to help you make the best use of all the open spaces in your garden. In a well-designed garden, every square metre of vacant ground will be floored, furnished, planted and even decorated for maximum enjoyment. The first chapter begins with a detailed appraisal of the concept of the garden floor. After defining the terms, we look at how you can evaluate what you have, in the way of surface areas, and will show you how to take maximum advantage of any natural attributes or any existing features that have come with your garden, or that you may have installed in the past.

We will cover such important aspects as the scale and proportion of ground spaces, and their relationship with other parts of the garden, and will demonstrate

how scale can be altered to change the overall effect. Shape and layout – not merely of the spaces between principal features but of the entire garden – will be discussed here, too, since small changes in how things are arranged can have such a profound effect on the overall view and feel of the garden.

It will be important, too, to look carefully at planning, and to touch on how outline plans can be easily prepared, first on paper, and then tested outdoors, before firm commitments have to be made. Changeability is one of the great keys to successful design, and last minute changes often result from adapting a theoretical design to the actual site. It is so important, when completing finishing touches to your garden, to be absolutely certain that whatever you have decided to install will sit comfortably – not only with the remainder of the garden, but also with the house and even with the surroundings beyond your boundary fences or walls.

The focal point of this book is to be found in the main section, Chapter 2. Every likely garden floor material is considered in detail, by way of an introduction to a series of inspirational projects. As well as giving specific information on each project, there is plenty of opportunity to explore other aspects that relate to the materials used, and thus to adapt the projects to suit your own special needs. Design projects included in this book cover such garden floor materials as natural stone, timber, concrete, recycled materials, grass in all its uses, specialist aromatic lawns and such natural substrates as gravel and scree grit. As many different characters and styles are presented as possible, showing what a huge range of effects is achievable. And specific structure details, illustrated in step-by-step drawings and including measurements, are given so that these projects may be imitated as closely as you like.

Planting is a key element of every garden, and even the finest design is without value unless the planting is equally inspired. It follows, therefore, that garden floors, regardless of materials or situation, are also dependent on good planting. Patios, terraces or other social areas, for example, will need furnishing with plants, perhaps in containers, so that hard edges and surfaces can be softened with greenery and brought to life with natural colour. Plants may, of themselves, become garden floors, particularly if a living ground cover is planned. The whole subject of plants and their special relationship with the garden floor is therefore covered in Chapter 3.

Garden features will take some years to establish and to mature. Materials mellow, plants develop character as they grow older, and it is likely that your own needs and tastes will alter over the years, and therefore likely that you will want to make changes. But even something as apparently solid as a garden floor plays a surprisingly dynamic role. The likelihood is that you will be making either small or major adjustments to your garden floor as time goes by, so the final section of this book, Chapter 4, gives advice both on how to maintain your hard landscape – that is, the built or manufactured structures – and on how to get the very best out of the living part of the design. Plant care is covered in detail, along with tips on how to replace plants, how to prune and train, so that the beauty of the area is in a state of continual enhancement.

Whatever the present nature or condition of your garden floor, something can be done to improve it. This book aims to provide inspirational ideas and advice to ensure that you make the most of the ground space at the heart of your garden – the part that almost certainly defines its entire character. Just as you would re-carpet or tile indoors when necessary, maybe now is the time to give your garden floor some serious attention.

Chapter 1

Designing the Space

Consider a typical country garden in midsummer, not dissimilar to the one pictured here. Colourful borders erupt with exuberant growth, flowers and foliage tumbling in all directions. Walls or fences nearby might be furnished with a variety of climbing plants – rambling roses, perhaps, with honeysuckle and clematis in gently contrasting hues. A lawn, probably central, will run up to the borders on either side, and these are backed, in turn, by a hornbeam hedge to the west and a purple beech hedge to the east. The grass is neatly mown, but a smattering of white daisies and blue speedwell break up the monotony of the green sward. Oh, and let us place a small lawn tree – *Sorbus folgneri*, a North American species of whitebeam – in the middle of the grass and surround its base with a circle of broad, leathery bergenia leaves.

Planning Before You Start

The first step with any project involving the establishment of a new garden floor is to familiarize yourself thoroughly with every aspect of the garden you intend to develop. A sound understanding of practical constraints is essential, of course, but if all the design problems are to be solved and, more importantly, if the results are going to inspire and delight you, they must always contain a strong element of creativity. This process should always be undertaken slowly and calmly, for the best results.

The preceding page describes, fairly accurately, part of my own back garden as it was until five years ago. Pretty enough, but the lawn was, frankly, rather boring. The site was too symmetrical, with little to relieve the large central area. And yet, I loved the sense of open space and shied away from suggestions – offered by well-meaning friends – that the area should be further enclosed with screens or barriers of some kind to create a series of rooms opening to a long, narrow central vista. My solution, borne out of desperation, was far simpler. I paved half the lawn with stone and left the rest green. A pond, 2m by 3.9m (6ft 6in by 12ft 6in) and severely formal, was incorporated into the paving, offset, so as to leave a generously proportioned seating area which, now that there was no longer grass to cut every week, was perfect for accommodating a table and chairs and more recently, a Portuguese clay oven. You would not believe the transformation that such a change has made. But there is more...

An army of helpers arrived and construction took place surprisingly quickly. Thrilled with the rapid development of the pond and the laying of the paved terrace, I dashed upstairs to admire the view from above. To my horror, I discovered that the whole site looked wrong. Lines that appeared parallel at ground level were clearly not, when viewed from above, and it was obvious that the paved area was badly out of line with the remaining lawn. The borders now had a decidedly skewed look. Yet, in that blunder lay the solution to a design conundrum that had been concerning me. Having a natural dislike of the work churned out by classical

designers and their drearily repeated symmetry in garden after garden, I had wondered how I could develop a modern, original-looking layout which would sit comfortably with our 17th-century house.

The next step was really the only option open to me. I removed the east flower border altogether and turfed it. The west border was divided up into a series of different sized rectangular beds, divided by neat, gravelled paths, and the line of the lawn was re-cut to square it off, making one of the borders L-shaped. After the initial mistake, this was all monitored from above – no more errors were permissible – and the result was a garden formed from a series of rectangles with lawn, pond, borders, terrace, hedges and pathways all offset to avoid any suggestion of replication. From upstairs, the effect was amazing: just as in a Mondrian abstract 'landscape', the squares and rectangles all had an existence of their own, and yet the relationship between them was clear. At ground level, the whole garden was transformed. The pond brought wildlife – dragonflies began to visit the water on the afternoon it was filled – the different little beds allowed me to diversify my planting into herbs, a clematis border, a Mediterranean scree and even a tiny nod to Victorian style formal bedding in one of the rectangles.

The point of this anecdote is to demonstrate the vital importance of the garden floor. From a pretty, but somewhat bland piece of garden landscape, I had blundered into a transformation which has made the area quite my favourite part. And all because we changed the garden floor, altering the space, the shape and the arrangement of the blank surfaces.

LEFT *A neat and coherent design that works well in this relatively small and confined town garden. Several different yet complementary elements compete for attention. The 'cut-out' lawn is especially attractive.*

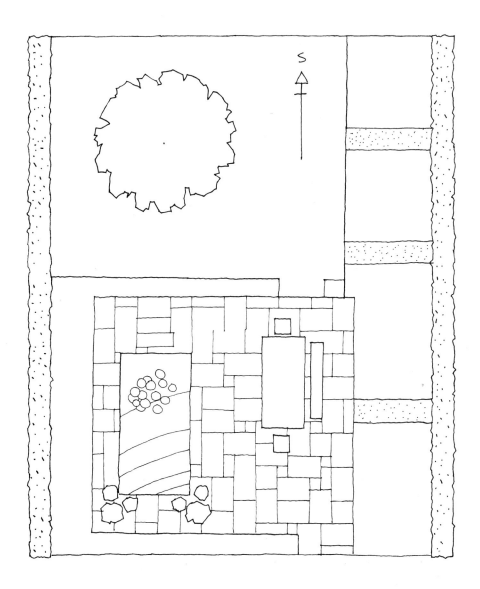

ABOVE *The rough, outline plan that I drew when landscaping the floor of my own garden. If only I had taken the trouble to do this before viewing on-going work from an upstairs window and realizing that it was all going horribly wrong!*

RIGHT *If you have only a small – or long and narrow garden, as in this case – it is still possible to make the floor the most attractive feature in the entire space.*

Make the Most of What You Have

Every garden site has its natural attributes. Usually, the more obvious of these point the way to a pleasing design, but assessing the full value of what you have may call for more careful observation than can be revealed in a brief inspection. Becoming familiar with every aspect of the place – warts and all – will help you to ensure that you make the most of what you have, whether this involves re-modelling numerous different aspects of the garden or simply working them into your new design.

Whether developing a garden from scratch, or adapting an existing design to suit your needs more closely, your chosen sites will have a number of natural advantages. It will be important to exploit these to the best possible effect, enhancing special strengths and minimizing any weaknesses. Any disadvantages, whether trivial or serious, will also have to be assessed and necessary remedial action decided upon before the final design is drawn up. It is a common human failing to accentuate negative features, but in almost every site there will be distinct advantages, and in the majority of cases, the 'pros' will outweigh the 'cons' by a considerable extent. Aspects that always merit special consideration are:

◆ **Gradient.** A sloping site provides extra scope for creativity. Areas that need to be level – such as for seating or socializing – can be terraced. This could result in a series of different levels, adding interest to the design and providing for a number of different functions. Thus, a seating area, water feature or planting plan might all sit on different levels. A level site, however, may give you a wide choice of dimensions.

◆ **Drainage.** Efficient drainage is essential, not only for developing paving or other surfaces that stay dry, but also for thriving plants. It will be essential to evaluate how well drained the site is, and if necessary, to install an underground drainage system before building anything else. Without proper drainage, your carefully planned new garden floor could be ruined within weeks.

◆ **Aspect.** Land that slopes towards the equator will always be warmer than land that slopes towards the pole. Buildings, walls, trees and hedges all throw shade and all, to a lesser extent, trap the sun on their lighter sides. A sun trap offers the natural choice for a seating area in cold climates, whereas naturally shady spots are preferable where cool seating is called for. All this may seem obvious, but when assessing a brand new site, it is important not only to be familiar with how it sits in relation to the sun's path, but also how much shade is thrown by surrounding objects – not only in summer, when the sun is high, but throughout the year.

◆ **Prevailing wind.** As with assessing aspect, it is important to have a clear idea of where most of the wind comes from. You also need to know which of the winds is more damaging. A light but freezing winter wind that has crept over a continent may be more damaging than a raging gale that brings warm, wet air from one of the major oceans. In my garden, for example, located in the East Midlands of England, westerly gales tear limbs off the trees, but it is more vital for us to create shelter from the east, since the continental winds from that quarter can drive frost deep into the ground.

◆ **Surrounding features – external.** Whether these are beautiful – distant buildings, hills or trees – or unsightly, it is important to be keenly aware of them, and to allow them to influence your design. Do not make the mistake of thinking that they will not be noticed – least of all by yourself. Efforts may be needed to disguise an eyesore, but it may be hugely to your advantage to make a beautiful skyline the backdrop to your garden.

◆ **Surrounding features – internal.** If your garden is already established, any changes you make to your outdoor floors will be influenced by what is already there. Even a new site, though, could carry a feature that will become part of the design. Natural rock, an old tree, the remains of a building – all these will need to be carefully considered. Of course, there is nothing to stop you removing old or unattractive items that you no longer want, as you develop your new external floors.

LEFT *You can transform a small town or courtyard garden with an attractive tiled design like this one. If the garden is most often viewed from above, such a design is particularly effective.*

RIGHT *If your garden is already well-established, with no identifiable 'floor' area, you could always build over the top of the existing surfaces, using decking. The wooden walkways and seating area in this garden contrast superbly with mixed plantings.*

Scale and Proportion

To a child, a flying aircraft has the appearance of a toy – far too small to carry passengers. It is all a matter of scale, and once the distance effect has been recognized, the mind compensates. How features or objects appear in gardens – and more particularly, how their size seems to compare – will also depend on their position in relation to other objects.

Having assessed what you have, the next and even more important step is to decide exactly what you want your garden to do for you. If you are a keen plant collector, for instance, you will want to maximize not only the area set aside for growing plants, but also the range of different conditions so you can grow the richest variety of species possible. If relaxation space is in greatest demand – be it a grassy area for the children to enjoy, or a focal point for adult socializing – then planted zones will have to be trimmed to make room. Decisions on how your space is to be used are yours alone, but whatever you decide, the open surfaces of the garden will still be of crucial importance in the overall design. Before getting involved with the series of detailed special cases that follow in Chapter 2, over the next few pages we will cover general terms that have an overall bearing on garden design and the choices you make.

As we have seen in the introduction, in most gardens it is not necessarily the structures themselves that are the key elements of a good design. Rather, it is the relationship they have with each other. Where they are placed matters, of course, but so too does the space between them. In a well-designed plot, all these features come together to create a rounded, pleasing story – just like a narrative plot – and it is in the creation of this that the floor space is so important.

Structures

One of the first considerations is scale. From the practical point of view, it makes little sense to construct outsize features in a tiny garden. A vast conservatory on the side of a tiny two-bedroom home would look ridiculous, and in a garden, a terrace that might grace a Palladian mansion will not look right if it dwarfs its surroundings. Equally, Ionic or Corinthian columns look daft if they comprise the portico of a one-car, flat-roofed garage. This is not merely a matter of taste – whatever that may be – but of retaining a sense of good proportion. A single broken classic column, as a garden feature, can look enchanting. Even an over-large statue, quite out of scale with its surroundings, can look good if it is introduced to jolt the senses, or to make an outrageous statement. But if you lose control of your general sense of scale and proportion, a mess is bound to ensue.

Open Spaces

Scale, as well as being important with garden buildings and structures, matters very much where open spaces are concerned. If the overall dimensions of your garden are small, the temptation will be to crowd too much into the available space and the resulting appearance could be cluttered and restless. But if you take

ABOVE *It is important to match the size of key garden features to the overall area of the garden floor. A huge summerhouse will invariably look ridiculous in a tiny garden.*

ABOVE *Use trees and shrubs to disguise eyesores and act as focal points, but bear in mind that if they are too big they will distract the eye from your new garden floor.*

RIGHT *The elements that make up this long, narrow garden are perfectly in proportion to one another, leading the eye down the garden and enhancing the overall perspective.*

care to preserve a big enough area to enjoy as an open space, you will be amazed at how many other features can be included in the remaining area. The sense of freedom that comes with the open area will more than compensate for crowded surroundings, because it provides a contrast between open, airy roominess and the busier, more structured surroundings.

Enclosed Areas

Where a garden is divided up into different 'rooms' or enclosed areas, the same rules apply to each enclosure. A generous open space will be more effective than a tiny one with clutter closing in on all sides, but variety makes for more interest, so the uses to which the open spaces are put can vary. Perhaps grass in one could be made to contrast with brick in another, or a gravel garden, or simply a border with low-growing plants.

Where screens that divide up the garden create long vistas, scale is even more important. At the end of a vista, for example, you will need something to look at. The clichéd solution is usually an urn or a statue. If it ends with a backdrop, such as a wall, you could use a moving water feature – perhaps a lion's head drooling or preferably, something more original and imaginative. Whatever you select as a vista 'stop', if it is too big, it will shorten the vista and will therefore reduce the impact. However, if it is too small, it will be invisible. Therefore pick the size with care. Also, use caution when choosing the surface of the path that leads along the vista. Make the pathway as wide and as much a feature in its own right as is possible, since it is this that carries your eye down to its end. The dimensions and shape of your garden will tend to dictate the scale and

LEFT *This impressive sweep of sheltered brick terracing works well in its own right, but the idiosyncratic, shell-like 'splashes' at each end add a real sense of drama.*

RIGHT *This little summerhouse is ideally proportioned to the surrounding garden and works as an effective vista 'stop' at the end of the path. In garden design practicality is just as important as visually arresting elements.*

RIGHT *This little summerhouse is ideally proportioned to the surrounding garden and works as an effective vista 'stop' at the end of the path. In garden design practicality is just as important as visually arresting elements.*

proportions of your open spaces. Long thin gardens, for example, need a completely different approach from square ones. If there is only room for a single long vista, it may be convenient to connect any open spaces with the one central path. If you pay careful attention to the shape of the open spaces, you will be able to create a series of different points of view, each one having an interesting backdrop. That way, the interest level is increased because you are able to develop a series of different scenes.

Planting

Before leaving this section, it is important to give a little thought to the scale of your planting, as well as to the structures. Since woody plants – trees and shrubs – are as structural as walls or other edifices, it is important to get them to scale. Living landscapes, even in formal gardens, should retain a degree of naturalism. In the wild, vegetation grows in layers, rather like a lasagne: ground cover plants are overshadowed by low shrubs which grow under, or in front of, trees. A piece of open ground, in a garden, should have something in common with a natural landscape. Around the periphery of most garden floors, be they terraces, patios, lawns or

decking, will be space for low, compact plants – so useful for softening edges, and for bringing dead materials to life. Behind these, you can arrange skeleton or backbone plants which will give coolness and shade in summer and provide a tall outline in winter.

In a tiny garden, the trees and other plants can be smaller than in a big space, but do not overlook the value of

LEFT *A narrow, winding path will always lengthen the perspective of a garden* (far left), *just as making one wider, or setting it off in different directions* (left), *will have the same effect across the width of the garden.*

occasionally planting out of scale. A huge leaf or two, for example, can add an element of surprise in a restricted space. A tall, narrow tree, like an exclamation mark, can punctuate an open area, especially if it is out of proportion with the rest of the structures and the planting. When juggling with scale and proportion, knowing how far to go requires an instinct for what works, in a design, and what doesn't.

Shaping Open Spaces

Garden design contains a strong sculptural element, not only where structural outline is concerned, but also in the way that the horizontal spaces are arranged. When it comes to garden floors, the concept of shape is every bit as important as accurate measurement of such dimensions as length and breadth. Such physical constraints as size and orientation will influence your decisions, of course, but there will also be plenty of scope for developing the overall layout that most closely suits your design. One of the most important considerations is how to shape the open space you are working in so that it not only looks good in its own right but also maximizes the effect of the other garden features that surround it.

The size of an open space will tend to dictate what use it can be put to, but its actual shape is important, too. A rectangle, for example, may well be easier to use effectively than a square – it is harder to divide up squares, for some reason – and a perfect circle, though attractive as a shape, will dictate exactly what kind of design surrounds it.

Open spaces are used for a wide number of different functions and frequently the function tends to dictate the shape. Paths are linear, either curving or straight. Lawns can be almost any shape, creating a green sea that separates other features – island beds, buildings, terraces and so on. Patios or seating areas will usually have symmetrical shapes, and will frequently open onto lawns or be fed by pathways.

The style of a garden floor will depend not only on its function but also on the nature of the garden. A formal layout, which depends heavily on geometric shapes and symmetrical designs, will probably feature neatly measured floor spaces. They might be furnished with structures, edged with formal borders or bordered with hedging, all of which will help to give the whole design its sense of balance and graciousness. Care is needed, when designing formal gardens, to surface the open floor spaces with materials that blend comfortably with the structured layout. Too many 'rustic' or natural materials tend to dilute formality, whereas severe paving, topiary or plants in formal containers can enhance formality, especially if their lines are kept as clean and simple as possible. Lawns will be neatly mown, weed-free and have straight edges. With time, any newness or severity of materials will tend to mellow as algae, and eventually, mosses and lichens begin to grow on the fabric.

Informal garden floors will be closer to natural landscapes. Hard edges, right angles, perfect circles and sharp corners will give way to soft, sweeping curves (but make sure they are curvaceous, rather than 'wriggly'!), with irregular planting and structures placed less symmetrically. Natural materials such as rough-cut grass, gravel and natural stone paving will work well, in such spaces and there is more scope to include a wider

RIGHT *What was once part of a field has here been shaped into a superb tableau of sweeping gravel path winding through majestic mixed plantings.*

variety of materials. Planting, in and around an informal garden floor, can be as random and as crazy as you like, but care is needed to prevent the whole site from degenerating into a mess. It takes a deft touch to design and plant an informal garden to perfection, whereas most people find formal layouts somewhat easier to plan and to plant. In reality, of course, most gardens will feature elements of both styles. Front gardens, in particular, lend themselves to formal gardening, whereas the relaxed, naturalistic landscape may give more lasting pleasure and interest at the back, where there is privacy.

It is easy to differentiate a keen gardener from a reluctant horticulturist. The former never has a large enough garden; the latter usually complains that he or she has too much to look after. If you feel your garden is too large, the solution could hardly be simpler: move house. Nothing else will content you. If you wish you had more space, on the other hand, bear in mind the cunning tricks that designers can play, to use the land more effectively, and to give the illusion of greater size.

Juggling with perspective helps. By changing the dimensions of a rectangular lawn, for example, you can push the horizon back, or bring it forward. Making it slightly narrower at the farthest end creates the illusion of a longer distance. If you enhance this deception by policing the height of the plants, or of a hedge, you can fool people into thinking your garden is twice the size it really is.

Different levels also help to extend the range of possibilities. Terracing is a charming design feature, for not only does it create a series of different levels, it also develops differing habitats,

LEFT *The succession of brick squares in this unusual terrace visually enhances its size considerably. The surrounding plants add height, again increasing the sense of space.*

ABOVE *Formal planting for a formal style of house. The symmetry and angular shapes of this garden perfectly reflect the architecture of the building and its foreground.*

making the whole area far more interesting. Each terrace becomes a self-contained room, or unit, which you can treat differently, turning simple progress from one to the other into a voyage of discovery – almost!

The social area – patio, terrace, seating area, call it what you will – is your garden's heart. It is usually closest to the house and therefore most readily visible from the windows. This means that visually it is of utmost importance, not only in summer when in frequent

use, but also in winter when the rest of the outdoors might be a little forlorn. The patio floor, must, therefore, look handsome, as well as being able to take wear and tear from passing feet. It may have to be resilient enough to survive the onslaught of teenage parties, or worse, toddlers' birthday bashes. And it must be safe. Forget knobbly cobbles or slick slate pavers here, and go for rough-textured paving, or for durable decking. Think, too, about safe surfacing, with such materials as textured polyurethane.

In some houses, the patio is almost an extension of the interior. Your conservatory might open onto a wide terrace, for instance, or you may have large glass doors which, when open, do

away with any barrier between living room and garden. With clever design, here, the transition between indoors and out can be almost unnoticeable, making the area far more pleasant in winter, but enabling both indoors and out to be used to the full in summer. If colours and styles on the inside are picked up and replicated, or at least nodded to, outdoors, the effect is of a pleasing unity.

Though largely functional, pathways are also an important element in the beauty of your design. They lead to different parts of the garden, they create vistas, they separate one section from another and, in a plantsman's garden, they will also carry a population of low-growing, good-natured plants. In formal gardening, they will usually be clean and straight, or have geometric curves, and are best laid down with man-made materials. In previous centuries, the traditional path material was hoggin, a mixture of sand and gravel which, when compressed, developed a hard but porous, non-slip surface. Such paths would be at least a metre wide and have a steep camber, to assist drainage in a period when skirts were well below the ankle. Nowadays, washed gravel serves as well, and also has the advantage of being non-slip. Brick or non-slip paving work well, too, and come in an extensive range of colours, shapes and sizes.

Steps and stairways are also part of the garden floor and, when well appointed and pleasantly decorated, can become superb features. As well as connecting levels they make wonderful vistas. At the world famous Abbey Gardens, Tresco, on the Isles of Scilly, a series of stairways runs in a straight line directly across the main garden, crossing a main lateral almost at its centre. Every stairway is furnished with beautiful and exotic plants, and there is statuary to entice visitors up to the highest part of the garden where, when they turn, they are rewarded with a vast panorama of the sea, clustered with little islands.

Drawing Up an Outline Plan

Planning is everything. Even the most inspired of designers will be doomed to fail unless they have a clear idea of how things will work out on paper before turning the first sod outdoors. Thinking about the area for a while, before even beginning to draw up a design, will allow the whole concept to pass through a development period during which all the various possibilities are considered. At this early stage, having an open mind and brainstorming for ideas will ensure that the best possible solution is arrived at in the end. Once it comes to the actual drawing of the plan, don't worry if you are no Picasso – the important thing is to gauge reasonably accurately how different elements will interact with one another.

Ideally, a garden should be designed in its entirety on paper before the first piece of ground is turned over. In reality, though, most gardens evolve slowly over the years. Even if you have dreamed up the ultimate design – or commissioned a designer – from the outset, the chances are that you will be making minor alterations all the time and may well go in for some major changes when new ideas strike you, or when trends and patterns change. It will help, however, whether creating a brand new garden or overhauling an existing one, to develop clear ideas about its layout before you begin.

The practicalities of drawing up a plan have been made enormously easier by using computers. Even if you despise the 'nerd's' approach and prefer to draw everything up with paper and pencil, do yourself the favour of at least looking at some of the garden design software products. If you are an indifferent, or an untrained draughtsman, but have plenty of ideas, a computer will help you to provide clear and accurate plans. You can also juggle with otherwise fixed objects far more easily on screen than having to redraw whenever changes are made. Most general garden software packages carry plant dictionaries, practical hints and, being interactive, also provide the opportunity for you to build up your own files – all theoretical, and a poor substitute for real gardening, but fun on a wet day or those long winter evenings!

Whether you are working on paper or on screen, your best starting point is to draw up a hit list of what you want out of your garden. Do this first for the whole area, and then for specific sections. Once you begin to divide up the space, keep double-checking that the various sections, especially the open spaces, are the right dimensions to function as required. Make free spaces as roomy as you can afford and give a lot of thought to the shape, particularly of any internal enclosures, and of the free floor space within these.

Pay close attention to detailed needs. Obvious questions are: where furniture

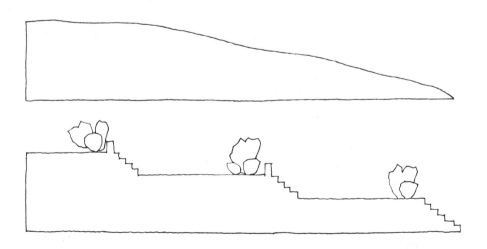

RIGHT *When you are drawing up your outline plan, start by viewing your existing garden design from an upstairs window of your house.*

LEFT *An outline plan will be vital for making any substantive change to the floor of your garden. These diagrams illustrate changing a sloping gradient to terracing. The principle here is no different from preparing a floor plan.*

will go? How the planting will be arranged? Will a water feature sit comfortably and safely within the area, or adjacent to it? It may also be worth asking yourself even more searching, fundamental questions. Answering such questions – the practical ones – will help you to decide what materials to use, as well as what size to make the open space.

There will be less obvious factors to consider as well. If you plan a barbecue, or outdoor cooking area, this should be situated downwind of the seating area, so that your guests are not suffocated by smoke and fumes as you prepare their food. If wildlife is a serious concern of yours, the chances are you will want to set up a bird feeding station, or at least install a bird bath. Unprotected ponds can be hazardous to very young children, so safety must be considered too, and, above all, check and double-check convenience and access from the house. Eating outdoors is glorious, but preparing food for outdoor consumption can be a nightmare, especially if the person carrying the food and drink has to make an arduous journey round obstacles and along crooked pathways from the kitchen to the outdoor table. All these things require careful thought before you begin realizing your design.

Much of the foregoing is concerned with designing an entire garden from scratch. But it is far more likely that you will want to adapt an existing one, and to develop a space or floor within an existing set up. Most of this book deals with specific garden floor projects on a scale that will slot comfortably into most gardens. Each can be copied or adapted to develop a discrete area within your garden, but there are some general

LEFT This garden floor has been carefully designed to line up symmetrically with the borders and hedges to each side, mirror the trellis at the back and also be framed by the arbour in the immediate foreground.

principles to such adaptations that should be considered here.

◆ **Make sure the idea is practicable**. You may need expert help in assessing the physical requirements of the site you are proposing to develop. Foundations or footings might be needed, especially on unstable soils, and you will need to ensure that the drainage is efficient. Where bedrock is fairly close to the surface, or where soils and subsoils are firm, less elaborate foundations are needed than on locations where the ground is unstable or where there is a high water table.

◆ **Be sure that you have selected the site and conditions that best suit your purpose**. This will depend, of course, on the use to which the area is to be put, but a site where seating is to be installed, or where people are likely to linger, will need to be sheltered, if possible, from prevailing winds, and will need to be sunny if the climate is cool, or shady in a hot region. Ideally, a seating area will need both sun and shade, and is generally far more convenient if sited reasonably close to the house. You will need to make sure the area is safe, too, and as private as possible.

◆ **Make sure it is pretty**. No one likes to sit in the shadow of an ugly object. Obvious though this may seem, it is surprising how easy it is to overlook an eyesore until after the plan has been carried out. Quite often, small adjustments to positions of seating, or the siting of screens or hedges can make a vast difference. Furthermore, a part of your design will consist of planting and furnishing the floor space, and will therefore, of itself, become a beautifying process. It is not likely that you will get everything right first time, so be ready to make further changes as you settle down with your new design. An open mind is a definite advantage with such projects!

◆ **Decide on which materials to use**. A number of factors will influence your decisions as to which materials are most suitable for the garden floor you have set your heart on: surroundings, your personal preferences, cost, availability of materials and, in some regions, local planning requirements. Unless you have already made up your mind, make sure you keep as many options open as possible and explore every possibility. If you cannot make up your mind, consult family and friends before going ahead with major purchases of materials.

◆ **Budget the plan**. Hard landscaping can be extremely costly and, unless good quality materials are used, the results can be very disappointing. If you are working on a limited budget, remember that all operations can be phased over as long a period as you like. Deciding on priorities will help you to get the best results, especially if you plant long-term trees and shrubs early on, and get the main, central garden floor – whatever form it may take – set up as soon as possible. Other embellishments can then await their turn.

◆ **Think about the planting**. Planting, or soft landscaping, is the most mutable of tasks. You can juggle with living plants to your heart's content, provided you only move them when dormant, and as long as they receive adequate aftercare. Even relatively mature trees will stand transplanting, but the older they are, the more difficult the aftercare once they have been re-sited. Try, therefore, to set up the bones of your background planting from an early date, but juggle about with the interplanting as much as you like. And remember that containers are a great way to shift plantings about without disturbing roots. Additionally, if you choose a hard landscape for your new design, then containers might offer the best planting options overall. They can add considerable visual interest.

Matching the Design to the Garden

The design of a new garden floor – however startling or innovative it may be – must rest comfortably in its surroundings, whether contrasting or harmonizing with the rest of the garden. Existing features, especially those that are the most prominent, will therefore exert a strong influence not only on the shape and structure of the garden floor, but also on the kind of prevailing mood it creates. Shapes, colours and textures – of both plants as well as materials – will all need to maintain a relationship with those of their surroundings.

The terms 'in sympathy with' or 'in keeping' are often used by planners when contemplating new building or landscaping projects. Keeping the design of a building – or a garden for that matter – harmonious with its surroundings is desirable, not only in terms of styles but also of materials used. That is why it is so important not only to be familiar with every aspect of your garden, but also to have a profound understanding of what it is about the design that makes it so effective. You will already have assessed what you have, in terms of aspect, local topography and climatic conditions, but it will also be necessary to evaluate any new project in terms of how it will sit with the rest of the garden.

Special attributes, to any potential site, will exert enormous influences on how your design takes shape. Some are so obvious that they are impossible to miss. Others, though they may be less apparent, still present wonderful opportunities. You might even see some of them as disadvantages, until they are turned on their heads and made to work for you and your design.

A natural water course – stream, river, spring or just a pond – would be seen by almost everyone as a wonderful advantage, providing scope for a huge choice of special features, perhaps including fountains, waterfalls, rills or even a small lake. But the benefits of an unusually high water table are less easy to identify, bringing as it does, drainage problems and the risk of dampness where it is least needed. However, a high water table, even if there is neither stream nor pond nearby, would enable a natural water feature to be created, or a natural bog garden to be laid out. There are plenty of ways around the dampness problem when laying a garden floor! Pages 68–71 cover a feature on decking, for example, an effective structure for raising an outdoor floor above ground level, thus keeping furniture, fittings and people high and dry. And, if connected to a series of boardwalks, decking can be used to develop pathways suspended just above the vegetation, offering a new and interesting point of view.

Natural rock formations can also be hugely valuable, especially in gardens where bedrock comes up to, and even emerges above, the soil surface. Any steep hillside site is likely to be rich with natural rock but even if it is not, it will look perfectly in keeping if large pieces of stone are introduced into the landscape from elsewhere. Sandy or gravelly

LEFT *There is no point in trying to impose a formal, structured floor design on a garden that is already dominated by rugged, wild plantings and emerging bedrock.*

landscapes are easy to enhance with extra gravel surfacing, so that the sense of naturalism is retained, but made more practical for planting, or for walking over.

Any existing garden structures will also need to be evaluated and worked around, or altered. Steps, walls, screens or fences could all feature as an integral part of your garden and are bound to figure in whatever further projects are planned. Your choice of floor materials will be influenced by such structures, and it is worth giving careful thought to how you can maximize the value of such assets – and minimize the effect of less attractive features – when you develop your ground floor.

With any new project, it will stand you in good stead to pay very close attention to the surrounding scenery that lies beyond your garden. If you are lucky enough, for example, to have beautiful rural views running up to your boundary, consider incorporating these landscapes into your design, or rather, 'borrowing' them for use as handsome backdrops. An Elizabethan garden I know in Lincolnshire, east England, for example, has been aligned so that its gate-house arch makes a perfect frame for Lincoln Cathedral, whose medieval architecture can be seen seven miles away. Where distant views are less sightly, you will want to plant trees or construct objects to mask them.

Obvious as it sounds, it will be essential to make a thorough evaluation of existing planting, and to ensure that this complements any new design project. Trees and shrubs, especially where they create the outline of a garden, will influence the rest of the design and wherever you plan to create a new floor space, be it lawn, paving, gravel, decking

RIGHT *The symmetry and relaxed formality of this floor design perfectly complement the surrounding plantings and general aspect of this garden, full of interesting contrasts.*

or whatever, you will need to bear them in mind. If you can leave the permanent planting undisturbed – especially established trees and shrubs – the redesigned floor space will blend in more comfortably or at least, will achieve a mature, established look more quickly. But if certain trees are in the way, and cannot be designed around, you may be better off removing them altogether and starting again. Developing a design around a mature planting takes skill, but can work far better than building a garden from scratch. However, if the plants compromise your design too much, or if it is difficult to see how you can make your new garden floor fit into the existing layout, do not be afraid of taking drastic action.

Herbaceous planting, faster-growing shrubs and climbers are far more easy to replace than trees, and will mature far more quickly. It is seldom worth spoiling the master plan of your design for the sake of a patch of Michaelmas daisies, say, or a hellebore, since such plants are quick to establish in new locations. What is important, however, is to adapt the design to suit the kind of planting you are likely to deploy. If you are fond of perennials, for example, you will need plenty of good, deep, fertile soil in beds of generous enough proportions to allow them to develop and multiply. If, however, you are content with a small number of shrubs, you can reduce maintenance needs by using weed-proof

membranes and a mulch, and, given a wise choice of plant species, can reduce the cultivable area considerably without the site looking too sterile or stark.

When choosing the materials for your garden floor, you will need to give careful consideration to the general style of your garden. If the existing layout is formal, with lots of straight edges, geometric borders and clipped hedges, an informal seating area or a rough grass flower meadow is bound to look at odds. Not that there is anything wrong with such a strong contrast – an aesthetic jolt can be right at the heart of a clever and original design – but it must be executed with panache. Oddly enough, in classic English garden designs, the opposite effect seems to work extremely well. The severe, structured designs of such great gardens as Sissinghurst and Hidcote are made more human and far more

ABOVE *If your garden is large enough, you can develop a series of different 'floors' that will complement the existing features and plantings in different areas.*

appealing by the random, almost chaotic nature of some of the planting. A formal brick terrace, or strictly symmetrical paved patio, can be made to look enchanting if summer flowers and foliage can be encouraged to spill onto the paving, perhaps even seeding in the cracks. Thus design and planting, formal and informal, come together to create the desired harmony necessary to make a good garden great.

RIGHT *As far as possible, endeavour to make your new design fit in with long-established trees, shrubs and other features, but do not be afraid to take drastic action if it is necessary.*

Matching the Design to the Style of Your House

In all but the largest gardens the dwelling is by far the most dominant feature and, whatever the layout, the chances are that pretty well every square metre of your plot will be in the shadow of the house it surrounds. Developing a close harmony with your building is therefore essential, if the design is to be pleasing to the eye and not jar with the ever-present bricks and mortar behind it. And the concept works both ways: as well as looking comfortable in its setting, with the house in view, the garden must also look attractive when looked at through the various windows. In many respects it is best to think of your garden as an extension of your house – an additional room, if you like – a concept which is currently very popular in garden design.

As well as matching the design of your outdoor surfaces to the rest of the garden, it is essential that whichever materials, dimensions or styles you use will sit comfortably with the design and fabric of your house. Frequently, it is a floor space area that actually connects house to garden. Pathways that lead to doors, lawns that run up to buildings, patios sited outside French windows – perhaps extending from a conservatory – are almost as much a part of the house as are any of the interiors. These must therefore be made to look attractive when viewed from indoors, and must also help to give your house more appeal when looked at from the garden or beyond the fence. As with all other aspects of design, this can be achieved either by creating an unobtrusive setting which amplifies the impact of the house or can be developed as an eye-catching

contrast, diluting the statement made by the building by distracting the eye away from it. Sometimes, the design of such outdoor features as pergolas, arbours or screens can be used as devices to mask part of the main building. Whichever path you choose will depend, of course, on how beautiful your house is to begin with.

The age of the house, as well as its style, is thus bound to influence your garden design. A half-timbered Elizabethan style building, for example, or a nineteenth-century cottage, is unlikely to look comfortable if it is surrounded by a terrace of modern ceramic cobbles in zany hues, or perhaps artificially coloured sands. Conversely, a stylish modern building could look incongruous if its setting is a romantic cottage garden or a replica sixteenth-century style knot garden. This does not mean that you have to enslave yourself to authentic period styles. It is important, however, to be aware that your garden's design is far more likely to succeed if there is, at least, an understanding of how architectural and

LEFT *A classic rustic house naturally looks best surrounded by a classic rustic garden, and any new garden floor being introduced to such a design should conform.*

landscape elements will marry together better if they have some elements in common.

But matching styles is not always quite as straightforward as it seems. As well as coming from different periods, building designs will have their own special ethnic style and, as such, will create a specific mood and feel within their surroundings. Most of the familiar ones are well known and clearly understood, so that typical vernacular dwellings, be they in Lisbon, Seattle or Sydney, will, have much in common. The architecture of each region, however, is further enriched by local specialities: for example, tiled walls in Portugal, beautiful weatherboarding in the western states of America and cast iron tracery work in old Australia. And in gardens, similar special styles prevail. English suburban front gardens burgeon with bright summer bedding; in Northwestern America, the Japanese and Chinese influence makes itself felt, with naturalistic water features and distinctly oriental looking rock work; in Australia, the suburban style has developed a distinctive local flavour, adapted to give the impression of coolness and greenness in a hot, dry climate.

When developing a new garden floor, therefore, it is important to harmonize with these special styles. Even though the uses the floor is put to may be common to all styles, the approach will be very different from one to another. Using appropriate materials will go a long way to finding the most comfortable design. Such designs as the timber deck garden, featured on pages 68–71, or the glass bead patio on pages 64–5, will work best with modern housing, built in a contemporary style. A period cottage, on the other hand, might look better graced

LEFT *The austere, sun-bleached decking that surrounds this house is perfectly suited both to its architecture and the prevailing hot, sunny climate.*

ABOVE *Gravel, dry stones and exotic plantings naturally complement red tile roofs and white walls, but would not look so good alongside a typical modern townhouse.*

by the herringbone brickwork which is explained on page 46, or with recycled materials. And if you wanted to go seriously Elizabethan English, try the knot garden on pages 80–3.

Think carefully about the colour and texture of your building materials. Most garden floors, even though they will be in gentle, muted colours, present relatively large surface areas and will therefore have a strong influence on the overall mood of the garden. Stone, brick and texturized concrete paving slabs are available in a wide range of shades and styles, so it is important to try samples of each of these, and to check that they will blend comfortably with the building materials of your house. Often, a contrast can be as effective as trying to harmonize the colours, but be on your guard for

clashing tones, or for differences in texture that can jar the senses.

Rules, though, are made to be broken – especially by creative and original designers! If your house was built within the last twenty years, does this preclude you from developing an eighteenth century maze? Of course not! Is the owner of a brick single-storey house, built in the 1940s, forbidden from laying out a classic Japanese garden? No! It is your garden and, provided you do not contravene any local planning regulations, yours to do with as you see fit. But it does pay to remember that whatever the design you finally decide on, things will slot in more conveniently and more comfortably if you take care to acknowledge the style and design of the house it surrounds. All that may be needed is a simple device – a trellis here, a discreet hedge there, perhaps a clearly defined space where a transition from one style to another can take place. It is difficult, and somewhat pointless to generalize, since each house and

garden can only be evaluated on its own special merits, but it is important to be aware of the influence the house is bound to have on the way you plan your outdoor designs.

This has been a brief look at the generalities of ground space design. It is difficult to go much further without getting down to specific examples, but before leaving the chapter, it is probably worth reminding ourselves of a few simple, but fundamental elements of design.

Firstly, we must never lose sight of what we actually want from our gardens. Fashions, and the desire to go along with the latest trends, often trick people into attempting to convert their gardens from something to be used, cherished and enjoyed into something to be admired, usually by others. Glossy magazines, which market themselves on being foremost with trendy new designs, often portray sumptuous interiors with photographs of rooms so over-dressed that it would be impossible to use them without knocking things over. One is treated to bathrooms with towels stored out of reach from the bath tub; kitchens unhygienically festooned with dried, dust-collecting vegetation hanging from racks on the ceiling; drawing rooms whose sofas and chairs look so uncomfortable that one would rather stand. And this nonsense has recently spread outdoors, so that at flower shows one sees prinked-up gardens with plants positioned where they could not possibly grow naturally, lawns that could not be mowed because they are surrounded by precipices, and so on.

Your garden, though, will be part of the real world, rather than a page from a pretentious glossy magazine! Its function is to provide an amenity that gives pleasure and recreation, as well as being delightful to look at. It will need to be cheap and easy to maintain, too, and above all, to be practicable, so that each and every function will work to its best ability.

Chapter 2

Choosing Materials and a Suitable Design

The floor space, or level area between features, is the most frequently used part of any garden. Whether it be pathway, patio or lawn, the area is certain to be well-trodden, and is likely to occupy a key spot. Choosing the right materials, and arriving at the best design for your purpose, is therefore more important than almost any other aspect of your garden's development. In this chapter we explore a wide range of materials and styles, in specific garden floor projects with differing dimensions and various uses. Whichever garden floor you choose, make sure your materials are practicable and easily installed. Above all, make sure that the design you select will be the one most likely to give you full satisfaction, adapting the concept specifically to your own special needs.

Stone

Stone is the most natural choice for paving. Whether it is recycled or newly quarried, the natural striations in limestone, the soft, warm colours and contours of sandstone or the bright texture of granite – even when it has not been polished or dressed – all help to create a comfortable, appealing surface. Expensive though it sometimes is, for most people natural stone will always be the first choice if the budget will extend to it. And it will certainly last....

Newly quarried, dressed stone is beautiful. Old building stone that has been laid for many years is even more beautiful. Even broken pieces of natural stone have a special quality that is impossible to imitate, even with the finest of manufactured composition pavers. In a garden few materials bring such a sense of maturity and stature, as does natural stone, especially if it has been skilfully installed.

The choice of natural stone is extensive, with colours ranging from white, through soft pinks or cinnamon and hundreds of shades of buff yellow or grey almost to black. The hardest-wearing stone is probably granite, which can run through almost every colour mentioned. In texture, granite is composed of coarse grains or crystals, but its surfaces can be dressed to a smooth, or even a glazed polish finish.

Limestone is probably the most widely used material, and may be oölitic – composed of billions of tiny fossil shells – or carboniferous. The former is a beautiful but rather soft stone, easily eroded and frost damaged, and more suitable for buildings than for floors. Carboniferous limestone is harder and more weather proof – York Stone is an example – and makes some of the best pavers. Its colours, however, tend to be more sombre shades of grey. Sandstone has a softer effect, often with attractive ochre or salmon shades. Slate, too, comes in some stirring colours, including blue, green, pink, purple or almost black.

Local stone, if your area has any, is likely to blend more convincingly with your surroundings than material that has been imported from outside. If there is a history of quarrying in your area, the chances are that your house is built, or at least dressed, with local stone, and this might look odd if your walls went down to a floor with a startling contrast. But the converse might also be true, for certain designs where a jolting contrast is called for.

Natural stone is extremely expensive. Expect to pay up to ten times the price for a dressed stone terrace as you might for one with concrete flags, and if you decide to use fancy granite or antique pavers, the cost will go up accordingly. There is also the important issue of conservation. In some parts of the world, beautiful landscapes have been disfigured by excessive quarrying, or surface extraction of stone. If you care about such things, make careful checks on the provenance of your chosen material, or decide to opt for a manufactured alternative. Just to put the issue into perspective, it is worth reminding yourself that gravel, concrete, stone and clay for bricks have all been extracted from somewhere, with an inevitable cost to the landscape.

Artificial stone, if it has been well manufactured, never looks quite as convincing as the real thing, especially when first laid, but in a well matured setting can be almost indistinguishable. Better quality pavers are made in moulds which are precise replicas of old slabs, carrying all the small irregularities of pattern and imperfections of the natural material. Though made of concrete, they are usually surfaced with a composition made from ground natural stone, making them strikingly similar.

ABOVE *Beautiful effects can be achieved with real stone slabs of varying colour and tone, arranged in 'crazy' paving style.*

RIGHT *Stone comes in many different colours and hues, making it one of the most attractive and appealing choices for a new garden floor. However, it is often expensive.*

Decorative Pebble Terrace

Pebbles, cobbles or random fragments of natural stone can all be used to create decorative but hardwearing surfaces. Design can be as formal or as informal as you like, from symmetrically replicated patterns to something wild and zany.

The design opposite consists of a mix of cobbles and broken fragments, used to create a series of swirling patterns in a circular, central area with quite similarly decorated paths radiating out from it. To get things right, before you start on such

a project, it is essential to have a clear idea of how many pieces of stone you will need, of each colour and size. But if you are working with recycled material, or your supply is limited, it will be necessary to adjust your pattern to make use of what is available. You will need to engage in some mathematics, working out areas of individual divisions and, bearing in mind the size of stone pieces, quantities required. Remember that the divisions between the stones add up,

especially if they are to be mortared and grouted, rather than laid almost touching. But allow for a few extra pieces of each anyway, to safeguard against running short and ruining the pattern. If the mathematics seem too daunting, suppliers of such materials are often willing to assist with patterns, and will help you to arrive at the right formula.

Be aware, when using natural materials, of conservation issues. In most districts, it is illegal to collect weathered stones or pebbles from beaches or river beds. Double-check on the provenance of all such materials before use.

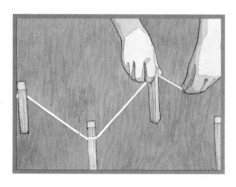

1 Mark out your pattern, using stout pegs and strong string. Be ready to adjust distances and shapes before hammering in all the pegs. Cut your pattern out of the ground with a spade, digging as evenly as possible.

2 Once you have cut out the pattern, rake and heel-down the ground until it is even across the entire design. Check for level by placing a straight piece of wood over the ground and measuring this with a spirit level.

3 Spread a layer of coarse sand (roughly 3cm (1in) thick) over the prepared surface and top this with a second, 6cm (2in) layer of sand and cement mix (proportion 7/1). Level and compact this down with a piece of wood.

4 Lay the pebbles, cobbles and broken fragments a few at a time and embed them gently into the dry sand/cement mix. Take care with the alignment of the stones, creating the desired patterns as you go.

5 Use a builder's trowel and a weak, near-dry mix of mortar to point up the pebbles, cleaning off as you go. Check for unstable stones as you work and, if necessary, use a little extra mortar to secure them.

6 Finally, before the mortar has had a chance to set completely, remove surplus grit with a stiff brush. The secret is to sweep vigorously enough to remove unwanted material, but not to dislodge newly laid stones.

Garden Chequer Board

This design is very simple and can consist either of two-coloured paving slabs, as illustrated here, or slabs alternated with other textured material such as gravel, cobbles or even soil which is subsequently planted up with such ground-covering plants as thyme or camomile. If the stones are recessed slightly – that is, sunk a little lower than ground level – mowable grass could be grown between them, resulting in a green and grey chequerboard.

Careful ground preparation is as important here as anywhere, since the stones will need to be secure enough to take hard wear and tear. A sub-surface of sand, gravel or hoggin will make for a stable base, especially if it overlies hardcore or bedrock, and will make the job of laying the stone pavers much easier.

If very large pavers are used, and if the ground is dead level and perfectly even, it should be possible to lay the pavers directly into sand without the need for

mortar. This will eliminate the risk of staining or disfiguring the pavers' surfaces with cement or mortar, but will mean that in time the pavers may move slightly. That, however, need not be seen as a serious disadvantage, since a terrace or a floor that has settled slightly, and has certain minor imperfections, looks more mature and therefore more pleasing and natural.

When laying natural stone, constantly remind yourself that it is easily spoilt, and though, once laid, it can be amazingly strong and hardwearing, it is often disappointingly brittle and susceptible to damage while being laid.

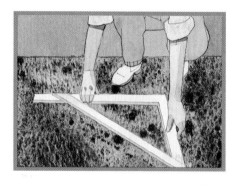

1 Mark out your pattern with a set of lines, making sure that the corners are absolutely square. Be sure, too, that you have calculated the precise area so that the stones are likely to be be correctly laid.

2 Level the ground roughly before driving pegs in at intervals, ensuring they are dead level. Use a spirit level to check, remembering to test levels in all directions. These will become markers for the final level.

3 Spread a layer of coarse sand or hoggin over the prepared surface and carefully rake it until it comes up flush with the tops of the pegs, ensuring a perfectly level bed for the pavers to be laid on to.

4 Place several dobs of stiffish sand cement mix where each paving slab is to be laid – some along each edge and one in the middle. A weakish mix – 5 or 6 of sand to 1 part cement – should be suitable for this.

5 Carefully lay each paver on top of the moist cement and, using the handle of a lump hammer, gently tap into place, checking constantly for level. Take care not to mark the surface of the pavers with cement.

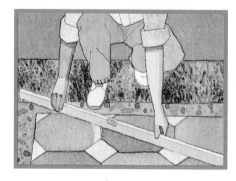

6 As the floor area develops, run constant checks for levels and for evenness across the pavers as a whole. It is far easier to correct mistakes before the mortar has set than when everything has hardened off.

Brick

Brick paving is easy to lay and lends itself to a wide variety of styles and structures. Building bricks vary widely, not only in colours and textures, but also in the shapes that are available. Nowadays, there is also a wide range of bricks that have been specifically designed for use as pavers in garden floors and pathways, rather than as materials for buildings. In areas where frost is prevalent in winter, these may prove to be harder-wearing and will, in almost every case, prove easier to lay. Before you select brick for laying as paving, be sure to decide whether it need be primarily hard-wearing – that is, for walking on – or just good to look at.

Baked building materials go back several millennia. The clay and straw blocks of the Pharaohs crop up in the Old Testament and those slim, tile-like Roman bricks can be found at archaeological sites all over Europe and the Near East. Today, clay bricks are just as popular for buildings, whether they be grand or humble, as they have been throughout the centuries.

As materials for constructing outdoor floors, bricks have a huge number of advantages. Provided they are made of the right materials, and correctly fired, they are almost as durable as concrete. Their colour range is wider than that of natural stone and the effect they create, when they are laid, is completely different from that of other materials. Different bonding systems create opportunities for a wide diversity of different patterns, allowing for a number of interesting effects.

Because bricks are light, and therefore easy to handle, bricklaying is less laborious for an inexperienced artisan than dealing with large, heavy slabs. Bricks, though, are more fiddly to lay than blocks, but if the levels go wrong, or the pattern develops an error, it should be a simple matter to lift some of the bricks and lay them again, since strong mortar will be unnecessary, provided the bricks' underlay is correctly prepared. (Details on how to prepare this are given on page 46.)

Bricks work particularly well for small areas, be they pathways, small yards or narrow terraces. Their small size makes them versatile for creating any number of interesting effects, but also makes them suitable for filling small corners, irregular boundaries or areas where stone or slabs would not fit in so comfortably.

In combination with other materials, bricks can be used to make a better finish. As linking seams between larger

ABOVE *Baked building materials now come in shapes other than that of the conventional, rectangular house brick, thanks to the versatility of modern technology. These wavy-shaped brick pavers are functional, hard-wearing and offer an aesthetic alternative to conventional herringbone or straight-on laying patterns.*

ABOVE *Bricks come in a variety of shades and hues and never look better than when more than one type are laid together. Abutting the bricks in different directions can add to the effect created by the different colours contrasting with one another. If they are durable enough, older bricks work particularly well when used in this way.*

slabs, bricks will provide visual relief on a paved area, but will also enable you to change dimensions, especially if you wish to make a more precise fit. Brick edgings to paved terraces give a professional finish as well as making the structure stronger by taking pressure off the outside pavers – usually the first to dislodge. To contain gravel within its allotted space, brick edgings make an excellent device, whether set on their sides or as a paved walkway. Bricks are also useful and decorative for edging borders, beds and pathways.

When purchasing your bricks, it is important to select suitable kinds, not only in terms of colour and shape, but also of the best quality. Cheap house bricks may not stand up to the rigours of cold winters when laid on the ground and could begin to crumble or perish after the repeated freezing and thawing of a normal northern winter. The toughest of all, and the most expensive, are known as 'engineering' bricks. These have been manufactured specifically to . withstand hard mechanical wear as well as climatic extremes. They are especially useful at steps or edges, particularly where vehicle wheels are pounding regularly at them.

Recycled or antique bricks can be suitable for laying on a terrace or path, but you will need to check on how effectively they will resist frost, and on their overall hardness. A useful test is to scrape the surface with a stubby screwdriver, or to twist a coin at its edge. If the metal scores or flakes the brick, it is unlikely to be suitable for laying on the ground. If the brick is unmarked, but the coin rim is dented, you could probably build another Empire State building with those bricks!

RIGHT *These hardy, bright pink bricks have been specifically designed for laying as pathways or for vehicular access. They might not be quite as appealing to look at as antique house bricks, but they will last!*

Herringbone Brick Terrace

This mixed herringbone and circular brick pattern creates a delightful effect which would be as suitable for a period building as with a modern design. The use of such bricks and patterns goes back several centuries, and if second-hand – or antique – bricks are used, the effect is even more attractive. Modern bricks will take a little longer to 'wear in' and to mellow, but you will be surprised and delighted at how quickly the whole area becomes established.

Good ground preparation is the first and most important consideration, ensuring that the floor area is even and either level or consistent in its fall. A layer of compressed hardcore will ensure a firm base, but you will need to add a layer of sand, approximately 6cm (2in) thick, above this, to give the bricks a firm, level, but slightly yielding bed. Rake this over repeatedly and keep checking for correct level.

Since the bricks are to be laid without mortar, they will need to be held firmly at the edges of the area, preferably with an edging strip. Edging strips may be made of concrete, laid and set *in situ*, manufactured kerbs, or could also be made with bricks. If the latter are used,

these – unlike the main body of brickwork – should be set very firmly into a shallow concrete or cement foundation so that the whole pattern is held firm. Objects within the area, such as manhole covers, will also need edging strips so that the brickwork can be laid neatly up to their edges.

Given the choice, select the hardest-wearing, most weatherproof brick available and go for a colour that you like and that suits the surroundings.

Where surroundings are also of brick, your paving may look better if you select a contrasting colour, rather than trying to match up hues, and making a near-miss. Clashing hues of brick red could look far worse than, say, blue-black or buff in contrast with a more traditional colour.

It should not be too difficult to calculate the number of bricks needed: divide the area by a single brick's dimensions plus a small percentage – less than 1cm (¼in) all round – to allow for the spaces in between. Be sure to arrange for a few extras, rather than run short. Any surplus is likely to come in handy anyway.

1 Once the site has been prepared, lay the edging strips. Make sure these are level and in the correct position. To keep the paving stable, edging strips should be held firm in a shallow concrete foundation.

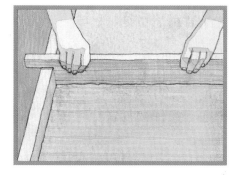

2 Bedding sand must be even. With a board cut to the edging strip as shown, work the sand until the surface is level. On wider areas, use a plank, ideally with two operators, and check constantly with a spirit level.

3 Stretch a line to ensure your paving bricks are correct to pattern. Then lay them, wearing gloves for protection from sharp edges, tapping them with a hammer handle to ensure they are stable. Check levels constantly.

4 Mark out corners, for filling in spaces along the edging strip, and cut them with a cold chisel. (It may take a while to develop this skill and make clean cuts.) Alternatively, use an electric angle grinder.

5 After a final check that all levels are correct, and that all bricks are stable, brush dry sand into the joints. If the site is level and the bricks correctly laid, it will not be necessary to use mortar.

Gravel

Gravel is the natural material of river beds, foreshores and mountain screes. It is not commonly found elsewhere in wild landscapes, but it can be used to develop a surprisingly natural look when used in an informal garden setting. However, gravel or stones of varied sizes can also look very beautiful when the design is more severe and formal – where it is often used to cover spaces between structures, or between formally clipped or pruned plants. Whichever way it is used, gravel is one of the cheapest and more versatile of all garden floor surfaces.

Gravel is considered to be modern and trendy but it has, in fact, been useful to gardeners for centuries. Elegant parterres were laid out with coloured gravels as long as 300 years ago and alpine enthusiasts have understood the benefits of growing plants in gravel since collections of such small mountain plants first became fashionable.

Where designs are liberal, with planting allowed to spill over onto pathways and seating areas, gravel is a wonderful linking substance, providing a firm, sure and dry footway, but also making an ideal substrate for the plants. The underlay in such designs will differ, of course, perhaps with hardcore beneath the areas to be walked over and soil under the planted zones, but the overall appearance is of a uniform surface.

For functional pathways, gravel is one of the best choices of surface, because it never turns slippery, even when wet, and because it drains so well. Fine gravel that has been mixed with a little clay or stiff subsoil, before being rolled down, will set to a hard-wearing, firm surface. Traditional pathways like this would be developed with a proud camber – or raised centre – to facilitate drainage on either side. If loose gravel is used for pathways, it is important to make the ground as level as possible before spreading the gravel, and to arrange for a kerb or some other device along the edges, so that the pebbles can be contained. If there is a slope, the gravel will tend to migrate downhill in time, and may need regular raking back.

Gravel makes an attractive colour contrast with the fresh greenness of lawns or rougher grass. Thus, pathways, if they are thoughtfully routed, will become design features, breaking up uniformity and providing comfortable eye lines. And with darker or lighter paving slabs, gravel will also give a colour and texture contrast, adding to the general interest, breaking up large areas into smaller divisions and sometimes helping to make drainage more efficient. Paths adjacent to fine lawns should be set lower – 6cm (2in) should suffice – so that stones are less likely to be kicked up onto the turf, hence jeopardizing the lawn mower.

When selecting gravels, bear in mind the information given on pages 28–31 about matching materials to your garden surroundings. By all means, explore the possibilities of selecting gravels to contrast with each other, not only in colour but in stone size, but think carefully before making your final choices, and study as many samples as you can find.

Artificially coloured sands and gravels are becoming available in some places and can make a surprising impact. The colours are clean, bright and wholly artificial. Vivid yellow, brooding violet, dazzling orange and bubble gum pink are a few examples, and there are even dappled mixtures that look more like ritzy coffee sugar crystals than dyed stones! The effect such colours would make might be wild and startling, but for imaginative designers who are not afraid to break the mould, they provide exciting opportunities to create something innovative and different.

LEFT *Gravel and small mixed stones have long been used in hot climates where grass and soft landscaping are hard to sustain. This Arizonan-style dry garden relies on gravel and pebbles for its overall effect.*

RIGHT *Gravel is plentiful, relatively cheap, hard-wearing and easy to replace. It washes clean in wet weather, looks good mixed with any number of different surfaces and comes in numerous different shapes, sizes, colours and hues. It is for all these reasons that its use has become so ubiquitous in gardens across the world in recent years!*

Japanese Garden

In this Japanese garden, preserving an authentic ethnic flavour depends on the precise placing of rocks, plants and other objects. An approximate understanding of the philosophy that underlies Japanese garden design will certainly help, but a deep working knowledge, though absorbing, is unnecessary.

Gravel, or smaller grit, plays a key role in Oriental landscaping, providing open areas between objects, but also often connecting them. In some landscapes, raked lines of shingle are almost like an ocean, connecting islands, but also isolating them. In terms of everyday usage, carefully contrived landscapes with deeply raked gravel are not very welcoming to walk on, since the patterns are easily spoiled by passing feet. Rather, this is a garden to contemplate, but will have strictly marked out routes where one may pass without upsetting the structure.

From the practical point of view, even the most esoteric garden needs to be maintained, and where weeds are likely to present problems, a buried membrane of weedproof, but water-permeable material is essential. Such a membrane will not prevent you from changing your planting plans, however, since it would be easy to pull the layer of gravel aside and cut through the membrane. It is important, however, to make sure that the growing conditions are favourable for the plants before the membrane and gravel are laid out. In any case, many plants will not look good set in the minimalist context of a Japanese garden.

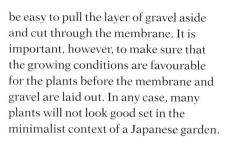

1 Ensure that the ground has been dug through thoroughly, that all perennial weeds have been removed and that the surface is firm. Rake the surface, and firm it down with your feet until the desired evenness has been achieved.

2 Lay a woven polypropylene sheet directly onto the surface. Tease out or pull out any wrinkles, tucking corners and ends neatly away. Cut off any surplus and make sure the sheet is securely anchored or tucked underground along every edge.

ABOVE *One instantly recognizable feature of nearly all Japanese gravel gardens are 'yin-yang' rocks, often characterized by enigmatic shapes and black veins that show through a usually grey/white stone colour. They look good against white gravel.*

3 Arrange your key plants. When satisfied with their positions, cut a cross in the sheet, and fold the corners back before planting. Before replacing the sheet, push any surplus soil underneath and then smooth the material around the plants.

4 Arrange rocks or other key features before spreading the gravel to a depth of at least 6cm (2in). Finally, rake the gravel to the desired levels, using a wide-toothed rake to achieve the desired 'corduroy' lines throughout the stones.

Mediterranean Garden

The popular concept of a Mediterranean garden tends to differ from the real thing! Most good gardens in the Cap Ferrat, say, or the Costa del Sol, are inclined to look luxuriant, with lots of tall, shade-giving trees, lushly furnished pergolas, containers and statuary, usually formally placed, but softened by relaxed, naturalistic planting. However, in Northern Europe and elsewhere, the term 'Mediterranean' refers more frequently to the use of drought-tolerant plants, rather than to a specific design style.

Authentic or not, however, gardens and garden floors like those illustrated here are becoming increasingly popular.

The number of plants that will thrive in such hot, dry conditions is considerable, and with a little careful planning the whole area can be made to look almost as alluring in winter as at the height of the growing season. Many of the Maquis shrubs (those from the rocky hills of the Mediterranean coastline) are evergreen and will provide a pleasing range of background hues in winter. Many have grey-green leaves, making a striking contrast, not only with the darker greens of, say, myrtles and hebes, but also with the clean, bright colours of such winter bulbs as species crocuses, dwarf irises or vivid blue scillas.

ABOVE *Gravel is a key constituent of Mediterranean gardens due to the drought-like climatic conditions that prevail for much of the year. This garden has a typical Mediterranean feel to it, in every respect.*

RIGHT *An extensive variety of plants will thrive in dry conditions, so a Mediterranean-style garden need never lack colour, texture or dramatic shapes. A garden like this one is harder to maintain, but worth the effort.*

In the gardens illustrated, the mixed areas of paving and cobbles or brick and gravel at the heart of the garden floors are brought to life with drought-tolerant plants slipped between the stones. Each specimen more than pays its rent in such plantings, providing colour and fragrance as well as helping to soften the hard, unforgiving lines of the structures. Laying gravel in the planting areas adjacent to the bricks or slabs, and under the plants themselves, will ensure favourable growing conditions by improving surface drainage and thus, keeping the necks of the plants dry, especially in winter.

Fine grits or gravels also act as mulches, helping to reduce the rate of evaporation from the soil surface and making it easier to get rid of weeds. A gravel and stone combination will also heat up quickly in sunny weather, helping the aromatic oils from such plants as thyme, rosemary and lavender to vaporize and provide their distinctive fragrance.

The major task to be undertaken in developing a free-draining, sunlit Mediterranean garden is to raise the levels of the pathways, so that the planted areas are as hot and as dry

as possible. In summer, such conditions will ripen the plants, ensuring plenty of flowers, but the warm sheltered conditions will also ensure the earliest possible start to plant growth at winter's end. Paths or thoroughfares that are frequently used must be stable and firm, so where necessary, reinforce these with extra hardcore, well compacted, before laying slabs.

If you live in a part of the world that does not naturally enjoy Mediterranean-style climatic conditions, tend your new garden floor carefully to maintain its authenticity. (See Chapter 4.)

1 Insert pegs at intervals along the length and width of the area to be gravelled, knocking these in until they are all at the same level. Check with a spirit level, and make any necessary final adjustments.

2 Lay hardcore, ballast or large gravel on the area, spreading this evenly until its upper surface is level with all the pegs. Smooth over any lumps or bumps and make sure the surface is universally firm.

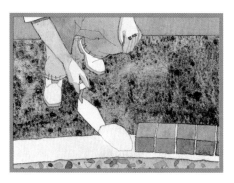

3 Lay a thin layer of mortar around the edge of the gravelled area and set bricks into it. Alternatively, lay slabs in amongst the gravel, again using mortar. Tap the bricks or slabs with a hammer handle to secure them.

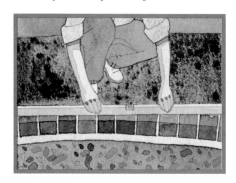

4 Once the bricks – or slabs – have been laid, point up the joints between them with mortar and use a spirit level to check levels. Adjustments are easier to make now rather than later – before the mortar sets!

5 Once the mortar has hardened and the bricks or slabs are fully secure, lay a generous thickness of gravel over the prepared area, up to the edges of the bricks or slabs. Rake the gravel until it is even.

6 Finally, introduce the plants, in and around the design. You may need to remove some of the gravel and hardcore and introduce a little compost, but if the correct plants are selected, they will survive.

Alpine Scree Bed

This garden floor is more closely geared to accommodate a plant collection than to use for sitting or walking through. One of the most attractive and imitable natural habitats to reconstruct in a garden is an Alpine scree. In the wild, these would be areas of mountainside littered with small stones or with grit, where eroding rock breaks up under the influence of freezing and thawing, of winter snow followed by spring water run-off. Plants that grow in these upland screes are adapted to a short growing season, often producing all their flowers at once in a spectacular display and setting seed thereafter surprisingly quickly.

In a garden setting, it is easy to adapt an alpine scree bed to carry far more than merely mountain plants. Short-lived, low growing Mediterranean bulbs, for example, enjoy sharing their habitat with such upland gems as saxifrages and gentians, adding to the beauty of the display. There are plenty of low-growing shrubs – from dome-forming daphnes to tiny, twiggy willows – and a number of mat-forming perennials which will provide wide patches of fresh foliage as well as a peppering of flowers.

The ground beneath an alpine scree bed can vary as much as you like – just as it would in nature – with hardcore under some areas but deeper, more fertile soil distributed elsewhere. If there is sufficient space, build up the levels by creating mounds or terraces in rough stone, scalpings or hardcore before developing the top surface.

1 Develop a plan on paper and buy rocks that are as close as possible in dimensions to your needs. Use pegs and string to mark out the area, showing the intended positions of the rocks, mounds and other contours.

2 Create the contours of your scree garden with mounds of hardcore. Place a layer of turf, upside down, over these to create the subsoil. If turf is sprayed with glyphosate herbicide, the grass will not regrow.

3 Position the rocks, but be flexible, making adjustments as you go until you have achieved the most natural looking scene. Large rocks may need anchoring with smaller stones to hold them stable.

4 Once all the major stone is in place, backfill the area with a mixture of garden soil, coarse grit and leafmould or well rotted compost. If you plan to grow acid-loving plants, this backfill must be lime free.

5 The first major planting is best carried out before laying the scree. Begin by positioning the Alpines in their containers and make adjustments until you are happy with the total planting design.

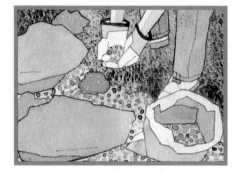

6 Apply grit with care, spreading it evenly under stones and round the plants. Aim for a depth of about 6cm (2in). Soil may disfigure the surface in places, after spreading, but this will soon wash through in the rain.

Concrete

Concrete may lack the romance of weathered natural stone, or the stylishness of modern decking, but as a cheap, convenient and easily installed surface there is little to beat it. Offering a high degree of elasticity – in that with its plastic content it can be made into whatever shape is needed – and durable enough to last for centuries, when skilfully installed concrete will outperform almost every other surface material available. The secret with this material is to alter its appearance so that it does not look like concrete at all. This can be done relatively easily, by pre-dyeing, painting or etching patterns into the design.

On the face of things, concrete may not be your first choice. But when you consider its versatility, durability and the ease with which it can be laid, concrete may present itself as a more attractive alternative than you first thought. And with a little ingenuity, you can make your concrete floor look almost natural.

The biggest advantage of concrete is that it is plastic, at least until it sets, so you can create whatever shape you want. If you are designing curving edges, steps and level changes, or if you want a flat surface to run up to an irregular boundary, concrete is the best solution. Most of the hard preparation work is in laying a hardcore foundation, and in constructing your shuttering so that the concrete will run exactly where you want it. And provided you have your levels correctly measured and double-checked, the concrete will find its own level. To ensure a long life, without cracking or shaling, concrete needs to be 'screeded' or vibrated, to help shake all the air bubbles out, and to make sure it is dense enough before it sets.

As part of the final screeding process, it is easy to build in special non-slip textures across the surface, making set concrete a much safer alternative to smooth flag stones which could become slick with moisture or algae in adverse weather conditions.

Small stones, cobbles or slabs can also be set into the concrete, to break up

ABOVE *Concrete can look grey and forbidding, but when textured with small pebbles, dyed to a pinkish hue and set into a pattern with bricks or other materials, as above, it can be an attractive, durable and much cheaper alternative to stone. Its malleable qualities make it an ideal surface for use in inaccessible areas of the garden floor.*

ABOVE *Concrete does not only come in an unbroken screed or in mock-stone paving slabs. Nowadays, it is possible to find a wide variety of different blocks and pavers that have been pre-set in concrete, often in different colours and textures. Here, light-pink concrete blocks contrast with grey blocks and brick shaped pavers.*

an otherwise boring surface area. An alternative is to build in a system of thin wooden lats, separating the concrete and giving – when the lats are removed – an impression of laid stone, rather than continuous concrete. If these are brushed vigorously with a wire brush, or a stiff bristle brush, as soon as the mix has gone off, the effect is further enhanced. Paint the new surface with a mix of yoghourt and tea, or sprinkle with liquid fertilizer, and the resulting growth of algae and mosses will complete the illusion.

Natural concrete, depending on the sand used in the mix, can be a rather forbidding, cold grey colour. But there are colourants which can alter the final hue, giving it a reddish, golden or buff effect. As an alternative, if the surface will take it, you could use paint to create a completely different effect.

The biggest downside to concrete is that once installed, it can be difficult to break up and remove. Make sure, therefore, that you have got all your levels right, and that all is as you will want it, before pouring the stuff out.

The other minor disadvantage is that you can seldom re-use concrete, once lifted, and so there is an attendant waste disposal problem, once you have decided to do away with a concrete floor. Pavers, on the other hand, can be raised and stored, or re-used.

Mixing concrete by hand, with a shovel, is very hard work, rather inaccurate, and very slow. If you can rent or buy a cement mixer – there are small ones readily available almost everywhere – your labours will be halved. If you decide to buy ready mixed concrete, make sure you have absolutely everything ready when the lorry arrives!

RIGHT *Stone-effect concrete pavers are increasingly popular for use as paths and garden floors. Cheaper and easier to come by than their real-stone equivalents, they still offer a choice of textures and colours.*

Decorated Concrete Terrace

When you first think about it, concrete seems pretty unromantic, more associated with modern institutions than with beautiful gardens – but concrete's great strength is that it can be whatever you want it to be. It can mimic stone to the point of total deception, it can be plastic enough to make curvaceous shapes and solid enough to build massive constructions. Its surfaces can be textured to any consistency from a polish to a deeply pitted face and can be dyed or painted to whatever colour you want. As for 'modern' – it isn't! Even the Ancient Romans used it.

The floor in the photograph to the right shows concrete at its wackiest. A hot, tropical garden with panels painted in glorious bright colours with exciting shapes that belong as much in a kindergarten playground as in a serious garden. But however extreme you may think the colours and styles, it does show just how far you can go with this versatile, and easily installed material.

The secret of success with concrete is good preparation. As stated before, the site *must* be perfectly level and correctly shuttered so that when the concrete is prepared and poured, it will flow to all the right places. When assessing how to concrete an area, remember that it is easier to work downhill, even if there is only a slight incline, rather than having to push the bulk of the material uphill all the time. Work out a plan of action, therefore, before the concrete arrives.

Bear in mind that it is generally easier to pre-dye your concrete rather than to paint it, if you require a colour effect.

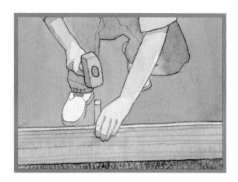

1 Erect shuttering for the entire area to be concreted. Make sure this is held firmly in place with pegs, that it is perfectly level and that there are no holes large enough for the liquid concrete to leak through.

2 Spread the hardcore base within the shuttering and pound down firmly, making a solid base. The idea is for the concrete to bond with the surface of the hardcore, but not to escape between loose brickbats.

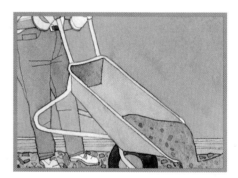

3 Begin pouring the concrete at one end of the site, gradually building up the thickness and roughly levelling the surface off. If the mix proves to be too stiff, add extra water to make it easier to work.

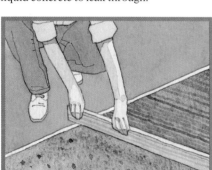

4 Screeding will help to drive out air bubbles and will ensure a level finish. The easiest method, on large areas, is for two workers to handle the screeding plank, pulling it to and fro in a gentle, sawing motion.

5 Any dips that appear during the screeding process will need to be levelled. Add small amounts of sloppy concrete at a time, and smooth these into the surface. Check evenness with the screeding plank as you go.

6 Final texturing takes place as the mix 'goes off' or begins to set. Vigorous brushing with a stiff broom will result in a roughened texture. Sweeping brusquely creates non-slip ridges, good for walking on.

Recycled Materials

In an age where such words as 'sustainability' and 'recycling' are on everyone's lips, the concept of developing a garden floor with recycled materials has an almost virtuous ring to it! Almost all flooring materials are reusable and many of them actually look more attractive when part-worn, or weathered, than when in mint condition. And as well as such obviously recyclable flooring as stone, bricks, timber or paving, there are a number of other fascinatingly novel materials to consider, including glass beads and even waste metal.

Voracious consumption during the past century has depleted the sources of a huge number of construction materials. Some, like natural stones, have become so scarce that their prices are prohibitive to all but the wealthiest gardeners. Furthermore, awareness of excessive exploitation of natural resources is increasing and the aim, for anyone who cares about our planet, must be to make better use, either of materials whose production is sustainable, or of recycled items.

The most obvious recycled products are those that have already been used as flooring materials elsewhere. Far from being second best, these are frequently choicer than their unused counterparts. Signs of wear will give the outdoor surface a sense of maturity and age and if the pavers or bricks happen to be mossed, or coated with lichen, so much the better. They may need careful handling, however, since the impression of age is easily spoilt if such materials are cleaned up. Stack them carefully, and try to avoid scuffing their surfaces too much. Above all, try to prevent cement or concrete from spilling onto their surfaces.

Because of their mature quality, used bricks or slabs will often cost more than new ones, especially if they have been recycled from period buildings. Finding them can be challenging too, particularly as professional builders tend to be secretive about their sources. Local papers sometimes carry advertising for reclaim companies, however, and these are almost always worth a visit. Always try to buy direct, rather than from a builder or builders' merchant, if you want to avoid providing the middle-man's profit.

A cheaper solution could be to recycle materials that have been junked. Broken slabs, old tiles, even ceramic shards can all be used to create interesting surfaces

ABOVE *Old cobble stones that have already been used as a flooring material will often look more appealing and will be considerably cheaper to acquire than brand new stones. The other great advantage of using such secondhand materials is that you will be sparing the environment by not exploiting precious virgin stone.*

ABOVE *These shaped pieces of slate, loosely set and framed by a brick edging, once adorned the roof of a derelict cottage. How refreshing to see them put to good use as an attractive and unusual section of garden floor, rather than simply being thrown away or left to rot atop a dilapidated eyesore.*

outdoors. If you have an artistic flair, and a magpie-like instinct for hoarding bits and pieces, you could develop a mosaic-like effect, perhaps even making pictures or patterns with your recycled materials. Just remember that the materials you select must be weather-proof, durable and reasonably easy to lay in mixed paving. Beyond these constraints, there are no limits at all and you can use whatever shape or colours you like.

In recent years, a number of industrially recycled or reconditioned products have appeared and can be used to excellent effect. Mulches, made from cocoa shells, bark chips, shredded timber or coconut fibres (coir) all create a certain effect when laid, not only to improve soil for plants, but as a finished outdoor surface. In certain Caribbean islands, old nutmeg shells are a popular material. They have the appearance of gravel but crunch much more loudly when walked over, and therefore advertise the approach of visitors (or, for that matter, intruders.)

One of the most interesting and attractive materials to appear in recent years is a kind of gravel made from recycled glass fragments. Dangerous though it may seem, the material has been modified by a special grinding process so that it can be handled, walked over or even lain on with complete safety. The effect of the process is to make the glass fragments opaque, when dry, but changing their colour and becoming transparent when wet. In a garden, this adds a delightful extra dimension. Various sizes of glass 'pebble' are available and, within the limitations of the original glass hues, a moderate colour range is supplied with mixtures of clear, brown, amber and green.

RIGHT *Admittedly not ideal for walking upon – and perhaps not very safe, into the bargain – these old washers and gaskets have been reclaimed from the scrapyard and put to unusual use as a decorative garden floor.*

Glass Bead Lawn or Patio

Small recycled glass beads can be laid as a loose ground cover, much in the way that shingle or gravel might be deployed, and will make a pleasant surface for taking light wear. One of the unlooked-for charms of such material is that it changes in appearance completely when wet. In dry weather, the beads are soft in colour, since their surfaces would normally have been ground down for safety, giving the effect of their having been sand-blasted. But after rain, the surfaces of the glass beads become slick and reflective, and their full transparency is regained, so that the original glass colour shines through.

Larger glass beads or pebbles can be used to create a mosaic effect, either in abstract patterns or arranged more intricately so that they create distinct shapes and figures. Though man-made, such materials are hard-wearing enough to floor a busy thoroughfare, or a seating area, and yet are highly decorative.

Ceramics, too, can be used in this way, and there are special ceramic 'pebbles' which have the same iridescent effect as a butterfly's wing.

Pebbles like these can also be blended or merged with other paving materials, or interspersed plants, to create interesting or varied patterns. They could be laid as small panels, to break up the monotony of a large paved area, or could be set into brickwork or slab paving to bring extra variety. They can also be used on vertical surfaces, as pictorial displays, or simply to continue a theme that might have begun along the ground.

1 Ensure a well-levelled, firm base, preferably consisting of hardcore overlaid by sand or sand and gravel. The surface must be entirely free of large pebbles or chunks of stone. Rake thoroughly for evenness.

2 Set plants into the design before laying mortar and glass beads around them. Select plants that will do well in the relatively hardy conditions that will prevail. Spread the plants evenly across the design.

3 Make sure the area is dead level, and then spread a layer of dry mortar over the surface with a spade. Do not allow the mortar to become wet at this stage. Be careful not to choke the bases of the plants with mortar.

4 Spread the glass beads evenly across the floor and around the plants. Alternatively, wet the mortar, mark out patterns using a trowel and set different coloured beads into a more formal design.

5 Water the glass beads liberally so that the dry mortar mix will 'go off' beneath and around them, holding the beads firmly in place. There is no need to water the design if you have set the beads into wet mortar.

6 Brush further sandy mortar down between the pebbles, to ensure an even firmer set. Keep off the new site until several days have elapsed, to give the beads plenty of time to bed in.

Wood

Wood is easy to work with, easy to repair or replace and, above all, is a natural product. As an outdoor floor covering it is not quite as versatile as stone or other paving slabs, but as a construction material, timber has more uses than almost anything else. Unlike stone or concrete, wood is inclined to rot or perish, unless properly treated and protected from the elements, but unlike any other material, wood is easy to paint, varnish, stain or simply to leave in its natural colour. If you are keen to create a naturally beautiful garden floor surface, look no further than wood.

Timber offers a range of uses in garden floors, from stepping 'stones' made out of sectioned tree trunks to carefully constructed decking or flooring. But wood can also be used to enhance a garden floor made of other materials, either by mixing it with those materials or by skilfully deploying it in the vertical structures that surround the floor, be they trellis, fencing, posts or pillars. Used in its natural colours, wood can blend seamlessly into informal designs, creating surfaces that are barely visible, or can make gentle contrasts with bolder outlines of trellis or fence. In artificial colours, either subtly stained, or boldly painted – but not blue – timber floors and structures make stronger statements and can be used to impose a stricter element of formality.

Recycled wood, even from such industrial sources as railway sleepers, can be made as attractive as the newest, smartest timber. I have seen an excellent raised, decked area built entirely from disused lorry pallets. They had been roughly planed and painted a soft but cheerful orange. This may sound awful to restrained gardeners, but it was a strongly lit, breezy seaside garden, and the colour worked well with the bluish silver of the foliage plants that surrounded the decking and the sea.

Railway sleepers are stout and strong enough to play important structural roles in garden design. What is more, they have been deeply impregnated with wood preservatives, and will therefore last for a very long time before rotting. As retaining timbers for raised or banked beds, they are excellent; as flooring they can be laid directly onto the ground and, provided the area is free draining, will last for decades. The resins and tar they contain can be troublesome, especially in hot weather, when it can ooze out, staining clothing and damaging plants, but the advantages outweigh this drawback in most designs.

Trellis structures built to surround and enhance floors – be they screens, obelisks, archways or simply wall claddings – can be decorative in their own right, even before they have been planted up. But it is important to remember that they are almost always more attractive when used as vehicles for climbing and wall plants, perhaps growing out of containers standing on the garden surface you are aiming to improve.

Block flooring and decking are alternative outdoor surfaces to paving or brick. Their main advantages are that they are softer, and therefore more

LEFT *Sawn planks in the form of decking offer a manageable and attractive alternative to other hard garden surfaces. It is essential to set the planks close together so that chair legs will not slip between them.*

RIGHT *There are few materials more natural or appealing to the eye than levelled old tree stumps or sections cut through tree trunks used as wooden pavers. Many garden centres now sell the latter, which look attractive laid in paths and floors alike.*

sympathetic in seating areas than are unyielding stone materials. Furniture sits more comfortably, and an entirely different ambience is created with wooden flooring. In areas of steeply sloping or uneven ground, decking enables a level floor to be created which will blend easily into the topography, and over marshy or boggy ground, a boardwalk can make a delightful feature, enabling you to get closer to the water plants without getting your feet wet.

It is essential that decking and other outdoor wooden structures are kept as dry as possible. When protected by paint, the life of some – but not all – timbers can be extended, but standing water, constant dampness or humidity will hasten rotting. With decking, spaces between the boards will assist circulation and reduce the incidence of rotting, but if these spaces are made too large, chair legs will slip through them, making the area awkward for seating.

RIGHT *Bamboo is increasingly popular for paths and small areas of garden floor. You do not need to invest in the more expensive king-size poles – standard bamboo sticks will do, so long as they are set close together.*

Deck Garden

Decking has become a popular and useful surface for garden floors and wherever the ground is uneven or sloping, providing the means of creating a warm, stable surface which is practicable for furniture and pleasant to sit on. As a means of elevating the floor level, decking is the simplest solution and probably one of the least expensive. Since wood is softer than stone, but no less natural-looking, it offers a pleasant textural alternative and, where different colours are wanted, wood makes an excellent substrate, not only for opaque surface paints, but also for an increasingly popular range of wood stains.

In damp climates, decking is likely to have a more limited life unless the timber has been properly heat treated with preservatives, and unless the whole floor is constructed correctly, with water or damp kept firmly at bay. Foundations will benefit, where practicable, from having waterproof membranes laid over them before flooring is fixed. Decking boards themselves need to be separated enough to allow air to circulate through the floor, but close enough together to prevent chair or table legs from slipping between them. Separated boards will also feel much cooler in hot areas, because any cooling breezes will be able to pass up through them.

Where decking is visible from beneath, it may be necessary to disguise the surroundings with trellis, or boarding of some kind. Trellis is good because it helps with the circulation of

LEFT *There are few better or more natural-looking ways of raising the level of your garden floor than by installing decking. These steps down to the rest of the garden denote a level of man-made terracing that could only enhance the visual interest and versatility of any garden.*

RIGHT *A spectacular deck garden, photographed on a damp morning in San Francisco. In wet or changeable climates – especially in warm regions – it is essential to treat wood thoroughly before laying it as decking.*

air, but also makes a handy vehicle for growing climbing plants. And if the decking is to be used as a seating area, it will be a natural choice for the climbing plants to grow up to the seating level and beyond, and to consist of a mix of gorgeous fragrances as well as handsome flowers.

Where decking is used to create boardwalks, the uprights that are driven directly into the ground will not only be subjected to considerable stress and strain from the weight of passing feet, but will also be more subject to rotting than those inserted, dry, into

foundations. Use the stoutest posts you can lay hands on, therefore, and make absolutely sure that these have been correctly treated with long-term wood preservatives. One excellent choice of upright posts would be railway sleepers, which are widely available from garden centres and salvage yards; but again, ensure they have been properly treated.

RIGHT *Decking can be used in any number of different garden contexts. The surface is traditionally used as boardwalks in Japanese gardens to traverse areas of raked gravel and yin-yang rocks.*

1 Space the main supports evenly across the area to be covered by the deck. They must be able to resist sideways movement, as well as downward pressure. Prepare shuttering to rest directly on the foundations.

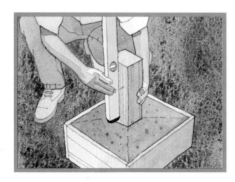

2 Bed the upright supports into the foundation, ensuring that each one is held vertically while the concrete is poured into the shuttering. After the concrete has been added, check the uprights again, with a plumb line.

3 Where decking is installed over sloping ground ensure that the upright support posts are dead level with each other. The illustration above shows supports both on level ground (top half) and on sloping ground.

4 Before anchoring the beams to the uprights, lay each one out, and check for levelness. If any uprights turn out to be proud, saw off a thin layer; if any are too short, build them up with extra timber.

5 Joists must be screwed or nailed to the beams at regular intervals, ideally every 60cm/2ft or so. Nails should be hammered in at an angle of roughly 45 degrees. Ensure that the nails or screws are of good quality.

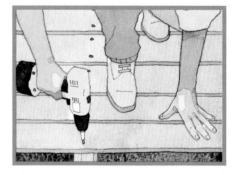

6 The decking boards must now be fixed, with two self-tapping screws per board wherever it overlies the joist. Complete the job by attaching side-skirt boards to hide the supporting structure below the deck.

Grass and Wildflowers

Grass is perhaps the commonest surface to be found in any natural landscape. Whether part of lush water meadows, impoverished rough pasture, roadside verges, waste ground or ocean foreshores, grass will always figure strongly. In some situations the turf may be cropped by grazing animals, or may be naturally short and fine; in others, long grasses can rear up at the height of the growing season to create impenetrable thickets, but almost everywhere you will find colourful flowers nestling in the green.

G rass is a living plant, but when planning garden floors, grass lawns can be considered as structural or surfacing material. Lawns are as viable, for floor covering, as any other material, but it is important to develop the kind of surface that will best suit your needs, and to remember that grass is a dynamic, living being, subject to wear and tear but, if properly looked after, able to repair itself.

To be very hard-wearing, lawns may need to contain coarser grasses than would be seen in the finest swards. Therefore, select your seed or your turf with care, choosing the right species-mix for the job. Grass selected for such special features as lawn mazes or grass pathways should be as hard-wearing as possible, and must be laid on free-draining but fertile soil. When such thoroughfares are over-used, especially in rainy conditions, there may be an excess of wear at certain times of year. Reduce this by employing some of the methods such as sinking paving or stepping stones, described on page 42.

Where grass is used as a substrate for planting, as well as to walk over, it will be important to develop a maintenance policy that enables it to perform as you want it. A flower meadow, for example, will need different treatment from rough grass that is planted only with late winter and spring bulbs. Flower meadow development is covered in detail on pages 74–5, but by limiting the number of blooming plants to certain seasons, you can develop a part-time meadow which, in summer, mows down to a passable lawn.

Lawns can languish in certain conditions, and if these become extreme, it may be difficult to achieve satisfactory grass growth. Shade is the biggest problem, since few grass species enjoy woodland conditions. Those that do are unsuitable for turf, so a deeply shaded lawn can never be hard-wearing and will often develop bald areas, especially if the shaded area is dry. Poor drainage is damaging, too, but can usually be corrected in ways described on page 108. Excessively free-draining, sandy soil can also inhibit lawn development, simply because it dries out so quickly, causing the grass to turn brown after a few dry days. Where such extremes are encountered, it might be more sensible to abandon the idea of grass altogether and select an alternative flooring material.

Grass is also attractive as a covering for special areas. Grass seating, popular in medieval times, is enjoying something of a comeback with certain designers.

ABOVE *Grass is a wonderfully versatile material that will work in conjunction with any number of other surfaces or borders. In this garden, the rampant, tumbling border shrub contrasts effectively with the perfectly mown sward below.*

The idea is to create a raised area – a bank, or perhaps the framework of a seat of some kind – and then to turf the surface. Although grass is the most widely used plant for creating the turf cover, you could also use aromatic, mat forming plants such as creeping thyme, or camomile. Such 'micro-lawns' need to be kept in trim by hand, of course, and would almost certainly require artificial watering in summer. It is interesting to note that in certain countries, such as Norway, turf was used in ancient times as roofing material for dwellings. For that matter, it sometimes still is. A turf roof for a summer house? Why not!

RIGHT *A perfect grass sward is a boon to any garden, but it will not necessarily fit your needs as well as other, hardier grasses that do not present themselves quite as attractively. What will your lawn be for?*

ABOVE *Many different garden floor effects can be achieved by planting the exciting range of grasses now coming on the market. This sedge looks good with bamboo behind it.*

Wildflower Meadow

Wildflower meadows are becoming increasingly popular, not only because of their ecological value, but also because they can enhance the beauty of an informal garden for much of the year. In autumn and winter their grass should be kept relatively short without being mown, allowing autumn flowers such as colchicums and hardy cyclamen to develop. Later, in early spring, a succession of bulbs will provide colour until such hayfield species as cowslips, salad burnet and ox-eye daisies take over. If hay is taken, these flowers must be allowed to set seed first. If not, later prairie species will follow, but whatever the regime, at least one annual cut will be needed to prevent shrubs and trees from developing and taking over.

The initial part of setting up a meadow – if you are not lucky enough to have a stretch of old grassland already – is similar to developing a new lawn. The ground must be broken and dug over, with any resulting lumps broken down to a fine tilth which will need levelling, firming and seeding. The one big difference between setting up a flower meadow and a lawn is that the former will not benefit at all from any attempt to improve the soil. Indeed, the more fertile the soil, the more successfully the grass will compete, driving out the wildflowers. Therefore, if your soil is particularly rich, consider removing some topsoil before you begin the process of levelling and sowing. Even bare subsoil will suit wildlings far better than rich loam.

1 Cultivate the area in exactly the same way as preparing a lawn. Do NOT add fertilizer or any other organic matter and do not attempt to improve the soil. The poorer it is, the better the wildflowers will perform.

2 Rake the ground roughly level. Work on any obvious or unsightly dips or mounds, but bear in mind that it is less important for wildflower meadows to be dead level or even than it is for fine lawns.

3 Firm the soil thoroughly all over with the heels. Rolling will not result in the desired firmness, but if the family can be recruited to dance thoroughly all over the surface, the task will be made easier!

4 Spread grass seed at one quarter the recommended rate. Sow wildflower seed in patches after sowing the grass, or introduce wildflower plants later. Avoid seed mixes that contain rye grass.

5 Rake in the seeds. If rain does not fall within 24 hours, irrigate the area with a fine spray. Where birds are abundant, spread a layer of netting, or a horticultural fleece, over the area until germination has taken place.

6 Plant bulbs or young plants with care among the emerging grass seedlings. Ensure that the ground immediately round each plant – to a distance of at least 15cm (6in) – is free of grass.

Ground Cover Planting

Ground cover plants carry the concept of a lawn or meadow surface one stage further. Because it is possible to use such a wide variety of plants – and to create such rich and original mixtures – the possibilities for creating delightful garden floors with weed-suppressing carpeting plants are virtually limitless. Foliage, especially on evergreen plants, ensures that the area remains fresh and green throughout the year while flowers pop up in small groups or in broad, bold drifts, coming and going in turn as the seasons roll by.

The most natural floor covering in any garden is a closely woven mat of plants. That is how outdoor floors tend to cover themselves in nature, and a garden, after all, should be a reflection of the wild landscape.

Living carpets can be informal, like the flower meadow described on pages 74–5, or can be as formal as the knot garden analyzed later in this section.

Non-grass lawns, especially those planted with camomile, penny royal (*Mentha pulegium*), moss or creeping thymes, are not as hard-wearing as conventional grass, but have the added advantages of being sweetly aromatic, and in certain cases, of flowering at some stage during the season, completely changing the colour of the lawn. Unlike grass, these lawns need close individual attention, which often involves cutting plants hard back, replanting sections and generally making sure that all the component plants are kept as healthy and vigorous as possible. Unless you have unlimited time, or plenty of spare labour, it is probably wisest to keep such lawns relatively small, but be sure to arrange seating on or near them, so their fragrance can be enjoyed.

Formal gardens, such as knot gardens or small parterres, work best with reasonably uniform plants filling the spaces between the convoluted hedges. These could be permanent – all the plants mentioned for special lawns would do well in knot gardens – or they could be replaced at intervals. Tulips, for example, look beautiful when massed in a knot garden, and can be easily replaced in summer either with coloured foliage plants such as *Senecio cineraria*, artemisias and purple sage, or perhaps with highly colourful and ubiquitous summer annuals, such as marigolds.

ABOVE *Camomile is an effective ground cover planting for both small lawns and parts of low-lying beds, as here. When crushed by hand or under foot, it releases a delicate, pleasant scent.*

ABOVE *Clump- or mat-forming ground cover plants can look delightful and provide a genuinely alternative garden floor. It is satisfying to realize that this is how many outdoor surfaces are covered naturally.*

ABOVE *The key to successful and interesting ground cover planting is to blend and merge different plants together in order to achieve the maximum number of different colours, textures and levels.*

ABOVE *Heathers will supply hardy, reliable ground cover colour most of the year round, and look particularly effective when mixed together in a variety of different colours, textures and heights. There are numerous different species widely available.*

Informal ground cover must never be allowed to become boring. When selecting a blend of plants, think of every season – not just spring and summer – and make sure there are beautiful combinations of foliage and flower, or other plant attributes, to brighten up your garden in every month of the year. Bear in mind that certain plants are natural choices as ground covers, not merely because they inhibit weed invasions but also because they look good for much longer during the year than does the average plant. Cranesbills, particularly the virtually evergreen *Geranium macrorrhizum*, are tremendously valuable, as are the spring and early summer blooming pulmonarias, whose basal foliage is renewed after flowering and persists all winter until the new flowers emerge. Creeping deadnettles are fine in shade, as are the periwinkles, but remember to dot them with bulbs for extended interest. On banks or awkward slopes, try some of the creeping cotoneasters such as *C. dammeri*, or, go for a bold selection of large and medium-sized grasses, especially kinds that will look good in winter as well as in summer.

In certain conditions, non-flowering plants may perform best as ground cover species. Many of the ferns, for example, can be blended to create charming, quiet displays in dense shade. Mosses, too, can be encouraged to grow among them, creating a cool, green floor covering. Creeping fern species include polypody, blechnum and *Polystichum aculeatum*. Mosses are harder to acquire, but if you decide to collect any plant – moss or otherwise – from the wild, do make sure you are not contravening any wildlife protection laws before taking it.

Thyme and Camomile Lawn

Grass is by no means the only plant material suitable for lawns. It is, however, the hardest-wearing, the easiest to establish and the easiest to maintain. Other lawn materials will achieve the same desired green carpet – with or without flowers, depending on the choice of plants – and can make gorgeous features. But they will not tolerate the constant passing of feet, heavy wear from kids playing ball games, or pollution by pets.

The most popular alternative to a grass lawn is camomile, but in very dry situations wild or creeping thyme might perform better. In early summer, this has the added advantage of producing masses of mauve, purple, white or pink flowers, as in the photograph opposite.

Camomile belongs to the daisy family, and has emerald green, aromatic, feathery leaves. The best variety for lawns is the non-flowering form, 'Treneague'. Since flowers almost never develop on 'Treneague', most of the plant's energy goes into vigorous leaf and stem production, making for a dense, lush lawn. It is also low-growing and reasonably tidy in its habit. In very dry conditions, camomile will tend to flag,

and after rain, recovery can be a little patchy, especially if parts of the lawn have become worn.

In very hot, dry climates, use wild thyme, *Thymus serpyllym*, in any of its more vigorous varieties. Since these plants flower profusely, you may want to create a patchwork of different hues by using such varieties as 'Pink Chintz', 'Russettings', 'Porlock', 'Album' and so on.

Both thyme and camomile need occasional trimming, and for this job, a lawn mower simply will not do! Scissors or shears and hard labour are the only realistic option – one-handed sheep shears are extremely useful for the task – which is why small thyme or camomile lawns tend to be a lot more popular than big ones!

Other alternative lawn plants, offering scent or colour, include pennyroyal, which is a creeping, aromatic mint; acaena or New Zealand burr; wild white clover – which fixes its own nitrogen – and, for cool, shady positions, mosses. (See the Oriental Moss Garden project on pages 84–5.)

1 Having thoroughly dug the ground over, preferably incorporating plenty of organic material and/or rotted manure as you go, rake the surface until it is reasonably even and level.

2 Firm the area with your heels, in a dancing or shuffling movement until the whole area is firm, but not so compressed as to impede drainage. If you have access to a large roller, use this after heeling.

3 Set out the plants so that they are evenly placed. There should not be more than 25cm (10in) between plants. Dig the holes and begin planting as soon as you are satisfied that the distribution is even.

4 Watering is crucial, not only at planting time, but again a few weeks later and thereafter whenever drought threatens. Water to soak the ground all around the plants, rather than merely sprinkling the surface.

5 As the plants begin to merge, and the lawn develops, trim lightly with two handed shears, or sheep shears. Never cut the plants too short, but trim as often as is required.

Knot Garden

Traditional knot gardens belong to 16th-century Europe, but the concept of small, compartmentalized beds separated by low-growing, convoluted hedges is as apt today as it was in Elizabethan times. The great parterres of such majestic 17th- and 18th-century gardens as Versailles and Villandry are nothing more than knot gardens on a grand scale and, in humbler, more vernacular garden design, a small area, edged or marked out in box and containing a modest bedding system, is a simplified modern derivation of the knot garden style.

An authentic knot garden would have criss-crossing hedges, giving the impression that the lines they form are knotted together. However, a looser, more modern approach is often adopted these days, using an abstract pattern with clipped hedges containing beds either of gravel, or of bedded flowering plants. These are changed on a regular basis, in spring for summer colour, and again in autumn for winter and spring displays.

It is important to choose a suitable hedging material for your knot garden. The compact, dwarf variety of common box, *Buxus sempervirens*, is the most popular for several reasons: its dark green colour makes a strong outline; clipping is only necessary once per year; and the plant, though slow-growing, is very easy to propagate. For larger hedges, and for corner pieces or centre plants, try the blue-green leaved *Buxus balaearica*, bay, *Laurus nobilis*, or even Portuguese laurel,

ABOVE *One of the great things about knot gardens is that they enable you to create interesting patterns on the floor of your garden. Infilling the lines of box or yew hedges with coloured gravel, bricks or bedding plants will add to the effect. These elements are easily changed and renewed from season to season, again altering the design.*

RIGHT *This small, enclosed parterre offers a good solution for an alternative surface. Lacking the traditional interweaving box hedges, it clearly shows a more modern, relaxed approach to knot garden design.*

Prunus lusitanica. Speedier, but shorter-lived alternatives include lavender – particularly compact varieties such as 'Hidcote', rosemary and santolina.

If you can spare the time, propagating your own hedge will save considerable expense, but to raise box plants from cuttings to suitable hedging size will take at least two years, and your hedge will need another 24 months to begin to look complete. A handy compromise would be to purchase a limited number of hedging plants, to set out the skeleton main frame of your knot garden, but to propagate your own plants for filling in the rest of the hedge later. No one says the whole planting must be completed within a season!

When laying out a knot garden, be sure to prepare the ground thoroughly, especially along the routes of the hedges. Imperfections and unevenness will usually manifest themselves in the hedge unless these have been ironed out, as far as is possible. On poor soils, work compost into the ground and, where the hedge is planted, sprinkle a little bonemeal along the bottom of the trenches and incorporate it thoroughly into the soil before planting.

Hedge aftercare is also crucial, particularly as any gaps or plant deaths will disfigure the hedge. Water thoroughly at the time of planting and again several times during the first growing season. If plant deaths do occur, these may be caused by a disease such as phytophthera. If this is so, remove as much soil as possible with the dead plant and incorporate new soil before planting up the replacements.

RIGHT *This unusual design demonstrates the versatility of knot gardens. The wavy, swirling troughs of box filled with pansies hardly conform to the classic Elizabethan style shown far right, but the principles are the same.*

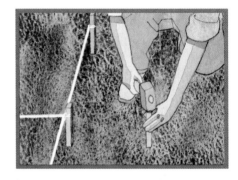

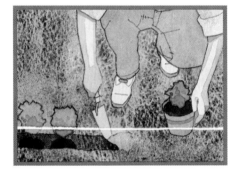

1 Ensure that the ground is level, even and weed-free. Drainage should be efficient and the soil improved with compost or rotted manure. Measure and mark out the pattern of the hedge, using pegs and a stout line.

2 Dig trenches to accommodate the plants' roots, add a little compost to the bottoms and arrange the hedging plants along them. Space box roughly 30cm (12in) apart. Ensure even placing and back fill. Water thoroughly.

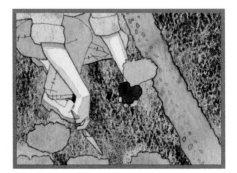

3 Trim very lightly in the first year, to encourage dense, twiggy growth. At first, only the stem tips need be removed. Gradually, as the hedge approaches its desired dimensions, cut back to these lines each year.

4 When planting in the knot, take care to prevent plants from overlying the hedge, as this could cause damage. Select plants which will form carpets, relying on foliage or flower to effect colour contrasts with the hedge.

5 Fill in the squares and patterns between the box hedges with coloured gravel, spreading it evenly around the plants set within the box. The gravel can be changed as often as you like, for added interest.

Oriental Moss Garden

Frequently, an area of garden floor begs to be fresh and green, but is simply too poorly lit to support conventional lawns and plants. And yet, many species of ferns and moss will grow even in the dankest and darkest of conditions. A moss garden is, therefore, a possible solution to a difficult gardening problem. Given adequate moisture, a little soil and some cunning design ideas, a moss garden carpeted with green and picked out with statuesque ferns and other plants able to survive in such low light conditions, could provide a more gorgeous display than the brightest of flower gardens, even if these are bathed in constant sunshine.

All garden designs need at least a few backbone plants, be they small trees or shrubs. In extreme shade, the choice will be somewhat limited. Few conifers will accept dense shade without growing leggy and weak, but certain laurels, particularly aucubas and bays, are surprisingly shade tolerant and, if well pruned and looked after, need not look dreary.

Mosses may be harder to find than ferns. Sadly, few commercial suppliers offer them, and if collecting from the wild you should take care not to contravene any conservation laws. However, if the conditions are favourable for mosses to develop, you will be pleasantly surprised at how many arrive and colonize the area voluntarily. You can hasten the spread of any that do, by taking small pieces off the parent colonies and replanting these, gently, where they are needed.

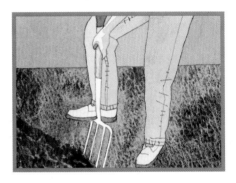

1 Work over the area which is to become a moss garden, digging out any remaining perennial weed roots and adding leafmould or garden compost to increase the organic level of the soil.

2 Develop the shape you desire for your moss garden, by raking level areas of ground or by mounding up soil to create hillocks and contours. Inverted turf can help to create the desired shape.

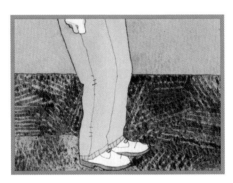

3 Firm down the soil, whether on the level or on a system of mounds. It is important not to compact soil so that it becomes impervious to water, but to make sure it is firm enough not to wash away in rain.

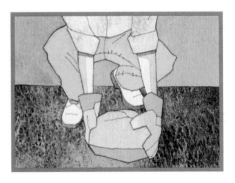

4 Place rocks, logs or large, dead branches in the desired positions. Take great care, when using old artefacts, not to rub off or spoil any natural mosses or lichens that might already be growing on them.

5 Plant ferns, plants and mosses. Small pieces of moss may be firmed down onto the surface of the ground where they should become established. You may need to weight some of them down with small stones.

6 As always with planting, water everything in thoroughly. Rainwater is always preferable to tap water, since it is unlikely to contain chlorine or lime residues. Some ferns and mosses prefer lime-free conditions.

Chapter 3

Decorating with Plants

It would be hard to imagine a garden without plants. Japanese Zen rock and gravel creations aside, gardens depend as much for success on planting as on artistic design. In fact, although inspired planting can often carry poor design – or even no design at all – bad planting will ruin even the finest design.

Plants do far more than merely decorate the hard landscape. Their functions are wide reaching and varied, ranging from structural – when they can create harder, bolder profiles than walls or buildings – to purely aesthetic, where they set the entire mood of the garden. Imagine, for example, the structural role that hedges play in dividing up the discrete rooms of such great gardens as Sissinghurst or Villandry. And then consider how, by filling the intervening spaces with bright flowers or with changing foliage, the spectrum is widened from rigid uniformity to natural variety.

Selecting Suitable Plants

The huge variety of textures and colours and fragrances that plants manifest can be composed to create a pleasurable sensual experience which will run through gradual changes, season by season. Above all, plants bring an otherwise sterile area to life. Sitting among greenery, in a living, changing environment, comes naturally to everyone and is known to reduce stress levels and create a genuine feeling of well being. So, wherever you plan to put your plants – whichever garden floor needs decorating with them – it is vital to select the right ones.

Practical Considerations

Plant selection begins with practicalities. It is as important to select plants that will thrive in the special conditions of your garden as it is to create artistic perfection. The latter will not happen unless the former constraints are understood. This is by no means limiting, however, since from the vast choice of plants available to gardeners there are bound to be varieties that will adapt to your garden's special conditions and will provide exactly the effect you want around your new garden floor.

Soil Type

Although most plants are very good-natured about where they will grow, some do better than others in specific soil types. If you are familiar with yours, you will be able to make your selections more judiciously. These are the main elements to ascertain:

◆ **Acidity or alkalinity.** If your soil is limy, you must exclude the small number of lime-hating plants from your shopping list – camellias and rhododendrons are examples – unless you plan to grow them in containers. Soil acidity is measured by recording the pH, a measurement of the number of hydrogen ions present. Precise definition is given in the glossary on page 124, but for now, all a gardener

needs to know is that pH7 is neutral and that any reading greater than pH7 is alkaline, and any less is acid. Soil testing kits are available, but in my experience tend to be unreliable, mainly because soil pH varies according to conditions, and because of the high risk of sampling errors. A far more reliable test is to peep over neighbours' fences and see what kinds of plants they grow. If rhododendrons are common in your area, for example, expect your soil to be acid. (Tips on how to improve soil, and how to alter pH are given in the section on maintenance, pages 102–122.)

◆ **Heavy soils.** These are the most difficult to work, but once in good heart, are among the most fertile. 'Heaviness' is caused by a high clay content, where soils have very small particles which tend to stick together, forming a dense material which is plastic when wet, but sets like concrete. Furthermore, clay soils are inclined to crack when they dry out. Good drainage is crucial with such soils, and if you can improve their structure by incorporating a constant

RIGHT *This pleasing combination of plants works well with the unpretentious, fairly basic 'floor' at the heart of this garden. The owner has taken pains to plant variety, whilst keeping overall maintenance low.*

supply of bulky organic matter –
compost, rotted manure, bark mulch,
leaf mould, lawn mowings, and so on –
your diligence will be rewarded. The
soil's natural tendency to retain water
will ensure that your plants suffer less
from drought and that essential mineral
nutrients, retained along with the water,
are readily available to them. At the same
time, the improved, crumbly texture of
the top few inches of soil will ensure
optimum growing conditions.

◆ **Light soils.** These are easy to work,
difficult to damage and warm up very
quickly in spring, resulting in early plant
development. Their disadvantage is that
they tend to dry out too quickly and to
become impoverished too easily. The
best way to prevent such problems,
strangely enough, is identical to the
treatment for clay soils, although this
time, the organic matter will be helping
to retain moisture, rather than opening
up the structure to let water through.
This may seem paradoxical, until you
realize how very different the structures
of these new soils are.

Prevailing Conditions

Besides knowing your soil, you need to
be as familiar as possible with the
conditions in your garden. The more you
understand these, the more unerring
your plant selection will be. Here are the
main considerations:

◆ **Aspect.** Obvious as it may seem, it is
important to know not only which parts
of your garden are shady and which dry,
but also how the degree of shade varies
according to season. Summer sun, for
example, might easily reach the area
behind a fence or wall which is fully

LEFT *In this garden, the combination of
dense upward growth, erupting above the
fat, round shapes in the box hedges, adds
immediate visual interest beyond the
plants themselves.*

shaded in winter. Large deciduous trees will throw dense shade in summer, but not in spring or winter, when a surprising number of 'off-season' plants can be enjoyed.

◆ **Wet or dry.** Apart from the level of rainfall, your garden will be wet or dry depending on whether the area is shaded by trees, protected from part of the rainfall by neighbouring buildings or whether, conversely, it receives more water than open ground, because of excessive run-off from elsewhere.

◆ **Exposed or sheltered.** Very sheltered spots are easy to foster tender plants in, but may be prone to frost. Exposed places need planting – not only with species that can shrug off cruel winds, but also to try to create living shelter screens.

◆ **Frosty.** Low lying areas, especially those that are enclosed, will be prone to damaging frosts, especially late in winter and early in the spring, when plants have begun growth and are highly vulnerable. Cold air flows downhill, and unless there is an escape route, will accumulate, causing damage.

Making Your Plant Choice

Having evaluated the conditions that prevail, the rest of the plant selecting process is pure pleasure! With planting, the fewer rules there are, the more fun you will have, but a handful of basic guidelines might make the choices open to you a little less bewildering. These three key maxims have always served me very well, and more importantly, have helped me to stay aloof from the silly style-mongering trends and short-term fashions that seem to come and go as much in gardening circles as they do with clothes.

◆ **Grow plants that you like.** This seems obvious, but unless you really love a plant, you are unlikely to look after it effectively. And when it comes to

arranging a planting, you are far more likely to hit off a happy plant association if you work with materials that you fully understand, and enjoy. Once your total planting system is completed, it will give you the greatest pleasure if every specimen is a personal favourite.

◆ **Grow plants that like you.** Every gardener wants to rise to the challenge of making a difficult, but gorgeous plant perform, but over the whole garden, the aim is for plants not merely to survive, but to thrive. And to ensure peak performance, you will have to select varieties that are happy and healthy in your garden's conditions.

◆ **Grow plants that like each other.** This may seem a bit pat, but good associations will only work if the plants that make them up are natural companions. This does not mean that they must be from the same geographical location, but merely from similar habitats. Mediterranean-style gardens, for example, can be enriched with plants from semi-arid regions around the world. Thus, European lavenders and rosemary look wonderful in association with South African gazanias or Central American portulacas. Woodlanders from North America, such as trilliums or smilacina, blend gloriously with Japanese hostas or with English bluebells and wood anemones.

◆ **Go for the best.** This is a rider to the three rules above, and so obvious that it hardly needs stating. But when space is limited, it is important to make sure that every plant selected pays its rent. Be sure, therefore, to select the best varieties – those with exactly the flower shape and colour that you most like, those with the cleanest hues, those with the most persistent flowering and those which present themselves to the best possible advantage. Look, too, for plants with desirable growing habits, for varieties with known disease resistance, and for plants that give more than a single display. This may mean a prolonged flowering season, beautiful autumn colour, fine winter outline, sweet fragrance, distinctive seed heads or any number of 'secondary' attributes. What is the point, for example, of selecting a rose that has no scent, or a plant whose spectacular flowers last but a day?

The Royal Horticultural Society's Award of Garden Merit is a good pointer for plants that have universal garden value. Increasingly, the AGM trophy symbol is displayed by plant retailers and is a valuable guide to the best choice of plants in almost every genus. You should not, however, make the AGM a required attribute. Many of the loveliest plants in my garden could never pick up an award, and yet they perform magnificently.

RIGHT *Even minimalist-styled Japanese and other gravel-based gardens need plants of some kind or another to really make them work. This miniature oriental pine contrasts starkly with the rock and gravel that surround it.*

Arranging the Plants

The art of planting is what makes a good gardener. Having a feel for which plants will grow happily together, and which colours will be specially effective – either deliberately in contrast with one another or in harmony – requires a combination of skill and talent. The part involving talent you are born with – some people just seem to know what looks right – but the skill part is learnt. How? Simply by observation, gleaning ideas from others, or better still, from nature herself. Experimenting with unusual plant combinations and even cashing in on happy planting accidents will all help perfect your skills as a good plantsman.

It isn't until you begin to plant up an area that you realize just what power the plants have in your design. Not only are you augmenting hard structures, but you are also creating specific moods and styles. You may not have a detailed masterplan on paper – indeed, it is often better not to be too firmly bound to a theoretical arrangement – but it is important to have in mind the sort of effect you want to create. Once you know where you are going with your planting, you can spend time building up to the desired effect. This will seldom come together in a single season, but within a short time, you will know how well the plants are likely to perform together, and you can begin making adjustments.

The first and most important consideration is to ensure that you have the right plants for the right spot. We have already covered the practical requirements, but it is also important to ensure that the selected plant, and the selected spot, will give you exactly the effect you want. A vigorous climber, for example, could look superb in its first three seasons, but might become an invasive nuisance thereafter, whereas a slow-growing one might try your patience for five years, but will look ravishing when it matures. It is important, therefore, to plant for the future, as well as for the current season. And in many cases, you can plant for both, using short-term species for the interim display while your choicer, but slower treasures are gradually finding their feet.

Plants for Altering the View

These are your skeleton plants, and could be as much a part of the structure of our garden floor as are walls or man-made screens. They may not, of themselves, be part of the floor, but their relationship with the horizontal surfaces is important. They will be visible all through the year, and in winter, when the rest of the planting is eclipsed, they will make key focal points. Evergreens are especially important, in this role, because they keep the garden fresh-looking in winter, as well as creating a neutral backdrop for summer flowers. But be careful to mix and match your evergreens with other outline shrubs, so that a good balance is set – with spring blossom, branches that are good for winter outline, and a changing foliage pattern through the year. Remember, too, that small outline plants, scaled down to be part of the garden floor, are as important in their function as the larger ones elsewhere in the garden, and that the same rules apply to them.

Hedges are included in this category too, as are other living screens, whether large or tiny. If you can, try to make them fulfil more than one function, or at least, make sure they are decorative as well as functional. When selecting hedging material, give consideration to fragrance, not only of flower, but of foliage, and if it is possible to snatch a bonus such as attractive flowers or conspicuous berries, go for that, too.

In-Fill Plants to Ensure Lasting Interest

These are the changing, seasonal mainstay of your planting system. Once the outline or structure plants are in place, these are the ones that will give you most scope for developing whatever special styles and effects you may want.

Much of the style will depend on the nature of the garden floor. A small paved area, for example, will demand a very different approach from, say, the free area that surrounds a decked terrace, or the planting needs of an informal gravel garden. In small areas, a limited group, or even a single plant, can carry as much impact as a massed planting in a larger set up. And in a small area, practically every leaf plays a key role; just as in chamber music, every note is crucial, whereas in a full orchestra, if one viola player hits a wrong note, no one but his neighbour will notice.

Planting for contrast is as important as planting for harmony. Create interest by selecting plants with distinctive foliage, and by aligning these with other leaves that strike a contrasting chord. The feathery softness of ferns, for example, can be enhanced with broad, leathery bergenia leaves, or with the cool, paddle-shaped leaves of hostas.

RIGHT *When planting alongside a newly-laid garden floor, think carefully about the effects the plants will bring throughout the year. Here, the mixed border on the left offers good seasonal variety and a strong contrast with the textural, shapely plants that line the right-hand side of the floor.*

Likewise, the grey, stiff habit of lavender plants makes a beautiful contrast with more lax perennials, or with old roses which are allowed to arch their flowering stems over the boundary hedge for a while. The number of rich planting compositions that can be created goes well beyond the scope of this little book, but do remember that your choice has virtually no limit, and that planting is something creative, to be enjoyed, rather than to worry over. Be bold, experimental or dashing in your choices. If your combinations fail, laugh at your mistakes, learn from them and have another go. Just as you must be prepared to make adjustments and improvements in the course of planning and laying-out your new garden floor, so you must be ready to try different plants and move things around until everything comes together as you would like it.

Here are some extra tips, for successful planting:

◆ **Labour saving.** Where a broad ground cover is needed, or if you are short of time and prefer not to spend too many hours prettying up your borders, go for labour-saving plants. This does not mean abandoning the planted areas to boring ground cover – unless a uniform, weed-proof green carpet is all you want – but it does call for thoughtful plant selection. Go for species that develop a dense, weed-proof cover, but which will not become a nuisance by swamping other plants in the area. Such perennials as the hardy cranesbills, heucheras, epimediums and astrantia provide more than one display and will merge to form a varied and beautiful green cover. Yet, they need very little attention, other than an occasional trim. Biennials, such as

LEFT *Most good planting schemes require a fine balance of colour, texture and form – ideally accompanied by fragrance. Containers and architectural plants are especially useful for achieving this balance.*

foxgloves, mulleins, honesty and sweet Williams that seed themselves are trouble free, developing successful colonies with very little effort. The display they provide, however, can be stunning, even in a restricted courtyard or a tiny seating area.

◆ **Pleasing other senses.** Fragrance is an important dimension in any garden, but since the majority of garden floors are either seating areas, or for recreation, or thoroughfares, fragrance is even more valuable. Try to arrange a fragrant plant or two to grow near where people sit. It need not even be highly visible, but could still give great pleasure to those who linger. Climbing plants such as honeysuckles, mixing with summer jasmine, over a bower, could help to create a charming feature, especially if there are a couple of extra climbers for winter bloom – *Clematis cirrhosa*, perhaps – and for autumn colour.

◆ **Sound and touch** are also valuable in a planting scheme. Plants that rustle – as some bamboos do – or that sigh in the breeze, like pines, help to give the garden its special character. As for touch, try planting bronze fennel, *Stachys lanata* or *Prunus serrula* and see if you can resist the temptation to touch, or to stroke those plants. You won't!

However carefully you plan your planting, there will always be a strong element of chance. Seedlings can self sow with surprising results, often making a better display than when painstakingly planted! I remember seeing the terrace of a beautiful Tudor house in southern England where the purple flowered *Verbena bonariense* had seeded itself freely between the large limestone flags. The effect was startling, since these flowers grow to a metre and a half (5ft), but because they are so thin and ephemeral, the impression was of a soft, purple mist hanging over the paving.

Containers and the Garden Floor

Containers bring extra choice to a garden. Not only are they impermanent, meaning that the changes can be rung with them as often as is desired, but they also create special features of themselves, almost wherever they are placed. A single urn, a cluster of pots, a planting trough or strategically placed hanging baskets all help to transform an area, perhaps bringing life and greenery to an otherwise barren spot, or simply boosting those plants that might already be *in situ*.

Most special garden floors, as described in the preceding pages, beg for containers. Whether they be pots or troughs, small raised beds or even wacky receptacles, containers transform paving, patios, terraces and pathways. Plants in pots draw attention to themselves more readily than when planted in open ground, especially when the pots are themselves decorative. In small courtyards or gardens that are completely paved over, containers present the only means of growing plants, and can be as effective when arranged in dense groups as can an entire border. But even in a garden where soil is plentiful and borders are abundant, containers act as a kind of horticultural garnish, standing in a strategic spot, making vista 'stops', or simply creating an excuse to grow some extra plants in different ways.

Here are some more advantages that containers bring:

◆ **They are movable**, either on a short or long-term basis. In cold climates, tender shrubs, such as citrus fruits, oleanders or *Brugmannsia* (formerly *Datura*), can be moved outdoors for summer, but placed under protection when the weather turns cold. Speedy displays, with sustained interest, are easy to effect, simply by rotating pots which contain flowering plants and foliage. I prefer to have a standing ground near my greenhouse for containers of agapanthus, pelargoniums, camellias and other seasonal plants, which are brought onto our terrace only when they are looking their best.

◆ **Containers provide** the opportunity to grow plants that would not survive your natural soil. In limy or chalky regions, for example, the only way rhododendrons, camellia and certain lilies can be grown is in lime-free compost in containers.

◆ **With containers**, you can make specific short-term displays – perhaps with baskets of flowering bulbs in spring, followed by bright summer annuals – which can be added to or reduced according to season, and according to the abundance of plants.

◆ **Gaps in borders** can be filled with containerized plants, either plunged into the soil, to be removed once the plants are over, or as features and focal points, to help pull the rest of the planting together.

Practicalities

In terms of everyday practice, container gardening is as easy, if not easier, than gardening in the ground. Practically anything can grow in a container, as long as it has enough room to develop roots, but large plants will be unlikely to achieve their maximum natural size. For containers to succeed, they need the following:

◆ **Drainage.** They must be well drained, with holes in the bottom to allow water to escape. Large containers should be placed onto special 'feet' which will lift their bases from the ground, thus assisting drainage. Broken crocks or polystyrene pieces should be placed in the container bottom.

◆ **Root room.** To grow properly, a plant needs enough room to develop a healthy root system; the container must therefore be large enough to accommodate all the roots comfortably, and to have extra capacity to allow for expansion. Pot-bound plants, with cramped roots, will look undernourished and will dry out too quickly. (Plants that have very limited root systems, such as cacti and succulents, are exceptions to these rules and will survive in surprisingly small pots.)

◆ **Cool roots.** Some plants will suffer if containers become too warm in summer sunshine, since their roots are adapted for cool, underground conditions. However, this problem is easy to overcome, either by planting round the base of the container, or by grouping containers so that the inner ones are shaded.

◆ **Frost protection.** Permanent containers, especially those made of earthenware or terracotta, may be

RIGHT *It is easy to add drama to any garden floor with the strategic placing of bright metal containers such as these, liberally planted with exciting blooms. Many different types of container are now widely available to buy, or why not recycle your own?*

susceptible to frost damage unless given winter protections. The problem is caused by the compost expanding, and also by water which has soaked into the fabric of the pot freezing, expanding and causing it to flake, or turn powdery. Choose only guaranteed frost-proof products, if they are to be overwintered outdoors in a cold climate.

Containers – the Choice

The choice of container is virtually unlimited. If it will hold compost, and it drains, you can plant it! Certain container designs work particularly well with composed garden floors. Which ones you adopt will depend, of course, on the style of the ground space you are developing, but some are almost universal, and will look lovely wherever they are set down or arranged. Here are some classic container types, with some ideas for planting.

Alpine Sink or Miniaturized Landscape

Choose a wide, shallow container for this. The best sink is the old-fashioned stone kitchen type, no more than about 3cm (1in) deep. Don't despair if you fail to discover a genuine antique article, since realistic copies are readily available and will soon mellow with use. To make them look old more quickly, paint these with a mix of yoghourt and strong tea, or sprinkle them with high-nitrogen liquid feed. Ensure the sink is well drained, and fill it with a very gritty, free-draining compost.

The choice of gem-like, slow-growing, tiny alpine plants is enormous, but you need to decide how much maintenance time you are willing to set aside, since some species are fiddly and demanding. House leeks (*Sempervivum*) and serums are neglect-proof, however, and capable

LEFT *Massed groupings of containers can look very effective, particularly if they are brightly coloured and of the same style and shape. The varying sizes of these ceramic pots adds an extra visual dimension.*

of surviving without ever being fed or watered! For a year-round display with moderate maintenance needs, try winter-flowering hardy cyclamen, miniature narcissus for spring, dwarf alpine pinks for summer and perhaps an autumn-flowering gentian. I prefer to cover the soil in my alpine sink with coarse grit, since this gives the impression of a genuine mountain scree.

The effect works best if the sink is raised above ground level, perhaps by as much as 45cm (18in) so that the small plants are brought nearer to the eye.

Large Pots as Planters

These are the standard, stock-in-trade items and come in a variety of shapes and sizes. A typical useful size, to stand on a terrace, might be 36–40cm (14–15in) in diameter and about 30cm (12in) deep. This would give enough space for, say, three pelargoniums, with trailing Helichrysum or lobelia as support plants. If you build up a selection of pots in varying sizes, you can make attractive informal groups and compose your planting to match the containers. Cool, blue themes, for example, could be achieved by mixing Scaevola, Swan River daisy, lobelias and white pelargoniums. Warmer blends might include nasturtiums, *Bidens ferrulifolia* or bright impatiens. There really is no limit to your

choice, but your containers will work best if you take great care with colours and match these, or contrast them with their surroundings on your garden floor. Keep your colours simple!

Chimney Pots, Baths and Other 'Wacky' Receptacles

Original ideas for containerized plants are often more effective than those which were once novelties but which have become cliches. Plants grown in old boots, lavatory pedestals, tyres and redundant wheel barrows are a touch passé as planters, but chimney pots and old baths, because they often have an intrinsic beauty whether planted or not, can be very effective, even when used to excess. Old-fashioned clay draining pipes, up-ended, make bizarre but handsome receptacles, especially if you can vary the sizes. Herbs such as thymes and marjoram do well in such containers, partly because they will tolerate low moisture levels, but also because regular trimming – to provide herbs for the kitchen – will keep them nicely to the desired size.

Permanent Containers; Winter Containers

The vast majority of container plants are for summer interest. Hanging baskets, window boxes and free-standing planters all tend to be subject

to a frenzy of summer activity, involving planting short-term species which will provide glorious colour for sixteen weeks but which would then prove to be hopeless for the rest of the year. And yet, the choice of plants for winter container gardening is almost as extensive as for the growing season.

Structure is all important for winter containers. In summer, you can get away with formlessness in your planting, because the colour and exuberance of the season will carry the display off. In winter, the outline is what matters, and your container needs architecture in order to work. Tall, narrow plants, such as *Cordyline australis*, or big, bold evergreens like *Fatsia japonica* can act as solid anchor plants. Their uncompromising shapes and bold foliage can then be offset with softer, gentler lines, of a sedge, perhaps, such as *Carex flagellifera*, or possibly a silver-leaved evergreen like cotton lavender. And these can in turn be contrasted with the bold, leathery leaves of bergenia, or the dark, miniature strap-like leaves of Ophiopogon. For flower colour, you can add winter-flowering heather, such as *Erica carnea*, along with early crocus corms and perhaps some miniature narcissus. When these fade, if you have planted them deeply in the container, you could introduce extra spring colour – perhaps primroses or violas – and then, when the frost risk has passed, try inserting a couple of bright summer flowers: *Bidens ferrulifolia*, or a trendy pelargonium variety. Thus, a run of interest is sustained through the year, but the basic structure of the contained planting remains unchanged and should flourish throughout the seasons.

When deciding which containers to choose, do give thought to the power of simplicity! A single specimen plant – imagine an elegant Japanese maple – in a finely crafted pot can carry a greater impact, winter and summer, than a whole trough full of riotous annuals.

Colour

Colour stirs up the emotions. Reds and oranges are warm, passionate colours – glorious and exciting for some people, but disturbing and unpleasant for others. Blues and white create a cool, sometimes chilly effect, whereas soft pastel pinks, mauves or creams are restful to the eye. Everyone has their own special favourites among colour combinations, but whatever your personal feelings might be, it is important, when planting, to understand as much as possible about colour and its meaning generally in life as well as specifically in the garden.

Before leaving this chapter, we should spend a few moments thinking in colour. In a garden floor area, as with everywhere else whether indoors or out, the colour scheme is one of the main ways in which you can create exactly the mood and style that you want. As any visual artist knows, colours cause varying emotional reactions. Strong, hot colours quicken your pulse; soft pastels can be calming. Red will always stand out above everything else, whereas blue tends to disappear. Complementary colours such as green and red, when they are placed close together, resonate – you can almost see them dancing before your eyes – whereas harmonious colours such as pink and purple blend almost seamlessly together, creating restful mixes.

Making Colour Work For You

Once you understand how colours work together, it will be easy to deploy them so that they provide exactly the effect you desire. The commonest error is to overdo the flower power. If there are too many strongly coloured blooms all massed together, the naturalistic effect is lost. In an interior, colours are entirely under your direct control; outdoors, you are not taming nature, but compromising with it, and the predominant natural colour of the landscape is green. This is not uniform, of course, but a series of green hues that vary widely, and that change hour by hour, month by month. And when you plan your colour schemes, it is essential to bear all this in mind.

Here are some more thoughts on making colour work for you:

◆ **Plan.** Decide well in advance what general colours you will want. There is no need to work out the scheme to the last leaf and petal, but it will help if you have a pretty clear idea of the general hues. Think, say, warm oranges and golds, or blues – or restful, soothing pinks and mauves.

◆ **Keep it simple.** The more extensive the range of colours deployed, the bigger the likelihood of making a mess rather than a composed picture. There is no need to be monochromatic, or to restrict yourself to limited colours for the whole area, but simple themes will always carry more impact than a mishmash.

◆ **Match plant colours** to their surroundings. The colour of the materials in and around your garden floor will influence your plant choice. This does not mean that you must labour for hours – finding exactly the leaf or flower to go with the particular shade of external paint, or the hue of your paving – but it does require thought. And it is easy to make mistakes: a double pink ornamental cherry against red brick can look frightful, if the colours clash, and yet can be gorgeously enhanced by a background of natural grey stone. The soft, purplish blue of wisteria never looks finer than against the honey-colour of old limestone.

◆ **Match colour to light conditions.** Pale shades work best in low light; loud colours perform best in sunshine. In shady sites, always select plants whose flowers are pale in colour, or white, since these shine out more prominently than do bright, intense hues. Even in strongly lit areas, the inclusion of a few pale colours, though they may look washed out by day, will keep the border looking beautiful late into twilight, when deep red or cobalt blue will have completely disappeared.

◆ **Use colour to jolt the senses.** A single flower, or a block of one strong colour, can make an exciting focal point, when placed near a seating area or beside a garden floor. In a Spanish-style patio, for example, where walls are painted pure white, a single splash of vivid red geraniums will carry more impact than would an entire mixed border of blooming perennials.

As a further means of sustaining interest, consider arranging for colour transformations throughout the year. You could develop a hot, restless effect in spring, for example, with strong yellows and stirring colours which could give way in summer to gentler, more restful hues, returning to gold and russet in the autumn. Spring-flowering shrubs, short-term bedding plants, carefully timed perennials and, of course, bulbs, can all be used to ring the changes through the year.

RIGHT *Good colour combination is all about subtlety. You do not need to mass garishly coloured annuals to achieve a strong effect: far better to chime discreet colours into the predominantly green background.*

Chapter 4

Maintaining Your Garden Floor

Most garden floors need little maintenance, once they have been installed. Paving, concrete and gravel will almost look after themselves, if well constructed, and most pathways are easy to keep clean and serviceable. Living floors, be they plants or grass, need a little more attention and at certain stages may call for a general overhaul. However, being aware of the prevailing conditions in your garden should have helped you to choose the best materials for your hard landscapes, and the most suitable plants. The purpose of this chapter is to help you foresee any potential problems – and to nip them in the bud – as well as to give a brief rundown of routine maintenance jobs, not only with the hard landscape but also with the plants and planting schemes.

Maintaining Hard Landscapes

The main consideration with the maintenance of hard garden landscapes is that any structural problems that present themselves – movement, physical damage, dislodging of pavers – should be addressed before they get worse. Sometimes, immediate action is necessary. But for most such structural repairs, spring or autumn are the most favourable times, because damage to the planting is minimal and frost problems are less likely.

This section is as much concerned with building and construction, as with gardening. If, like me, your handyman ability has never graduated beyond a six-inch nail, or a length of farmer's string, you are unlikely to get too deeply into bricklaying, wall building or major reconstruction. There are, however, simple troubleshooting measures and running repairs that can be accomplished quickly and easily, even by the most inept craftsman. There are also certain precautions which will help to minimize maintenance problems.

Keeping Water Out

Water is the biggest single cause of damage to man-made garden surfaces and structures. In areas where frost is prevalent, this risk is hugely increased, and where the differences in temperatures are most extreme – such as on a south-facing site – the destruction is accelerated. It is important, therefore, to ensure that your garden floor, whatever its construction, is efficiently drained. Any drainage holes in patios, or water escape routes in wall bases, must be kept clear and free so that water can pass through without backing up. Wherever puddles form on paving, weather damage is likely to follow.

If problem areas arise with drainage, you will need to rectify them. Parts of paved areas that have sunk, forming natural gathering places for water, can be repaired by lifting and relaying some of the pavers. Low, surrounding walls should have been constructed with anti-damp membranes, but old ones can act like candle wicks, drawing moisture out of the garden floor and evaporating it through their surfaces. In the process, mortar all around can begin to perish and the fabric of both the wall and floor start to crumble. The process of decay is inevitable, but it can be slowed down by minimizing damp, and by keeping the frost out. Re-pointing the mortar will help to make such walls waterproof, but it is even more important that their tops are protected from rain and snow, either with coping stones or roofing material. An old stone wall in my garden had shed its pantile ridge years before we arrived. As an emergency repair, we spread a uniform skim of thin concrete all the way along the top. This has arrested deterioration and the wall is in as good condition today as it was 24 years ago. In many cases, the same principles will apply to garden floors.

Running Repairs to Paving, Brickwork or Stone

From time to time, a paving slab can become loose and begin to teeter. As well as being annoying, this could develop

RIGHT *If they are properly laid in the first place, most stone, brick or concrete floors will not present too many problems. However, watch out for frost and keep the area as clean as you can.*

into a hazard, especially if there is a proud edge. Individual pavers, or small groups, are usually easy to re-lay in these few simple stages:

◆ **Carefully tease out** the loosest slab, before doing anything else.

◆ **Investigate** the cause of the problem. If the foundation cement has perished, or if the base has become unstable, remove any loose material and, if necessary, add back some hardcore and firm it down.

◆ **Prepare a stiffish mix** of cement and lay this in blobs over the base, making sure that the slab will sit a little proud of its neighbours when first re-laid, before tamping down.

◆ **Gently lower the slab** into position, tapping gently and evenly on all sides until it is snug with the rest of the paving. Clean any surplus cement from the area and, if the surface of the slab has become stained, wash the cement off carefully, preventing too much water from falling down the cracks and washing away the as yet unset support.

◆ **Allow cement to set** overnight, or for several hours. Finally, clean round the edges of the pavers, either grouting with extra mortar, to match the rest of your surface, or brush in coarse sand, if you wish to allow plants to grow in and out of the cracks.

Similar running repairs can be effected with other surfacing materials. Brick paving, if it has moved or become unstable, can be re-laid adding extra sand if necessary (see brick project on

LEFT *If garden floor brickwork begins to crumble or becomes unstable, it is easy enough to prise up individual bricks and re-lay them, using a little extra sand. If you have wholesale damage, you probably laid the wrong type of bricks in the first place.*

pages 46–7). You will need to discover, however, why the bricks became unstable in the first place, and address that problem before re-laying them. Cobbles set into a base without mortar will often begin to move, especially if they have been walked over to excess, but should not be difficult to reassemble.

Timber Treatment and Repairs

Decking and other timber structures are highly fashionable at present, and although they would not have the same life as stone or other hard paving, they are still durable. Decking is likely to last far longer in arid regions than in a damp, cool climate, but you can extend its life by selecting only timber that has been heat or pressure treated with preservatives at the timber mill.

The most vulnerable parts of a timber construction are those that come into constant contact with both water, soil and air. A fence post, for example, is always more likely to rot and break at ground level than above or below the soil surface. For wooden garden floors, therefore, be sure to use supports that have been heavily heat and pressure treated with bitumen or creosote, so that the preservative has fully penetrated the wood. You could also consider using protective sleeves for the posts, made of plastic or galvanized metal. A trick we used to employ with wooden gate posts, in my days as a farmer, was to coat the underground end with a thick layer of machinery grease, before inserting it into its hole.

The upper structures – joists and decking – are easier to keep sound, because they will be dry for most of the time. The better the timber quality, the longer the life, but regular painting with wood preservative, or with priming paint and topcoat will help to prolong the life of your timber. Make sure water can escape, and keep an eye open for damp corners, or areas where accumulated debris has slowed down the draining rate.

Wooden structures such as pergolas and arches can still be treated if they carry plants, but care must be taken not to use chemicals which could harm your climbers. Creosote is the least desirable, since it is toxic to most plants and will cause scorching, but there are other preparations that are kinder to green leaves. Painting, too, is an alternative, but if you are considering blue as a colour choice, remember that television programmes have resulted in everyone else having the same idea, and that in my opinion blue is horrible in a garden anyway, unless very carefully selected. How about black, white, ochre, khaki or deep or sage green – or maybe even bright orange – as alternatives?

The optimum season for maintenance work on wooden structures is the autumn. Not only will this ensure that the structure goes into winter in good repair, but it is the period when your climbing plants are least likely to suffer. Roses and clematis can be pruned hard at this time, and wall plants can be braced away from the timber and tied back with string while the repairs take place. Take care not to retrain them onto the wood until paint or treatments have fully dried.

Keeping Surfaces Safe and Clean

During winter months, paving can become slippery with algal growths and may be hazardous. Cleaning down with proprietary preparations or brushing vigorously with salt can help to prevent this from happening. If stone or pavers are persistently slippery, there are polyurethane coatings that have abrasive material added to improve traction.

Gravel which is never raked can become dull or dirty-looking with coatings of algae on individual stones. Regular raking helps to prevent such growth, and keeps the gravel fresh and clean. Weeds can be controlled in gravel, either by regular disturbance – raking or hoeing – or with weedkillers such as glyphosate.

Maintaining Soft Landscapes

Where soft landscapes are concerned, maintenance is not so much a matter of repairing as compromising with the plants. Routine cultural tasks such as pruning, weeding, training, dead-heading and feeding all crop up on a regular basis as part of the ongoing, and rather enjoyable, job of looking after the garden. Overhauling the planting, replacing lost specimens or introducing new ones are large jobs, but they too carry such a high level of creativity that doing them should provide nothing but pleasure.

Soft landscapes are dynamic, running through constant changes as they develop and mature. Sometimes they can be self repairing, but although there are ways of reducing maintenance time, soft landscapes always need more 'hands-on' fostering than do rigid structures. Plant care, the main and unending task, is covered in the final section of this chapter, but it is only possible to achieve optimum performance with your plants if your soil is in good condition.

Soil Improvement and Maintenance

We have already seen how best to prepare soils on pages 88 and 90 but soil management is an ongoing affair, needing regular, though infrequent treatments. Here are some regular routine tasks:

◆ **Composting.** Healthy soil is a blend of mineral particles, decaying organic matter, water and billions of micro-organisms. All soils benefit, therefore, from having their organic matter contents boosted. Incorporating compost – whether as a mulch, or digging it gently into the soil surface – will result in better plant growth and improved water retention. Composted weeds, prunings and dead plants will also help to return mineral nutrient to the soil, since these are released from the compost as it rots down.

◆ **Earthworms are important** too, distributing such nutrients about the soil, improving drainage with their burrows and helping to accelerate nutrient release by partially digesting the organic matter.

◆ **Regular mulching** will further improve moisture retention and is especially helpful during dry periods. Mulches should be applied when the soil is still moist, before winter's end. If applied very thickly, mulches also help to reduce weed growth – a distinct advantage – but remember, too, that such mulches will inhibit germination of desirable plants too. Thick mulches and self perpetuating colonies of annuals and biennials, therefore, do not go together.

◆ **Drainage problems** can be partially alleviated by incorporating bulky materials into the soil, or by building up raised beds. Such materials as grit, broken tiles or pulverized forest bark can all help to bulk up soil and assist drainage, if placed below the growing level of the soil.

◆ **Feeding** is almost universally overdone in gardens, and is seldom necessary

RIGHT *A camomile lawn makes a beautiful and fragrant garden floor, but it will require more on-going maintenance than most. The plants can become thin and straggly, and will need careful tending.*

where shrubs are grown in the open ground. Herbaceous perennials need no more than a very light spring dressing of any general fertilizer that contains nitrogen, phosphorus and potassium, or of well rotted manure, unless you are growing such gross feeding, exhibition plants as delphiniums or dahlias. Containerized plants are grown in more artificial conditions, and will need regular feeding, as discussed in the container section on pages 96–9.

MAINTAINING SPECIAL SURFACES

Gravel

Gravel is increasingly popular as a landscaping medium. It has been used for centuries as a substrate for pathways or for hard standing, but in recent decades gravel has become used more widely to create a beautiful, and easily maintained setting for plants. Whether part of a traditional Japanese-style setting, a mountain scree, or a modern, lawnless front garden, gravel has specific maintenance needs, and unless certain precautions are taken, a gravel garden can develop problems that are not easy to put right.

The method of laying deployed, and the size of individual stones within the gravel, will have some influence on how easy it is to maintain. Small stones, as found in coarse grit or pea shingle, are much easier to work through with hoe and rake than are larger pebbles. In nature, however, gravels are more likely to consist of assorted sizes, and it is often more effective to lay a mix of scree sizes rather than just one. Further, if you can scatter a few much larger pebbles or flints, the effect of a natural riverbed or mountain scree is enhanced. But rather

LEFT *Careful plant management is needed in a small Alpine garden like this one, to ensure that weeds do not predominate. Using different sizes of gravel and larger stones helps keep down maintenance.*

than a homogeneous mixture, your gravel should be laid in bold swirls of stones of contrasting sizes, and when it comes to maintenance, this effect can be spoilt unless you rake or hoe with care. On very small-scale gravel gardens, one size of pea shingle will work better, and is easy to keep weed free.

Weeding in gravel is less laborious than in soil, because simply moving the stones around – I use a shallow-set hoe for this – on a warm day, will cause emerging weed seedlings to perish without even having to pick them up for composting. The difficulty arises when desirable self-seeded plants are emerging among the weeds. If you wish to save all the desirable seedlings, hand-weeding is the only option, but it is seldom necessary to save every last one. If you make a compromise, it is best to hoe through areas that are going to look far more attractive if kept completely clear and to hand-weed in areas where a plant cover will be preferred. Do take care, though! Lack of ruthlessness, when dealing with volunteer seedlings, can result in a gravel garden becoming overrun by a handful of dominant species. In one of my gravel terraces, meadow cranesbills, in all their gorgeous colour forms, have teamed up with Californian poppies to make a stupendous display, but to the expense of everything else.

◆ **Use of a membrane.** Some landscapers prefer to minimize growth in their gravel by using a water-permeable but weed-proof membrane. Usually, this will consist of woven polypropylene – a tough, non-rotting material which will allow rain to pass through. The way this is used is to cut crossed slits in the membrane where perennials, shrubs or trees are to be planted. The corners thus created in the membrane are then folded back, the plant planted, and the membrane, and ultimately the gravel, replaced. The result is a scrupulously clean surface which needs no further maintenance other than an occasional raking over to prevent algae forming on the gravel. This is fine unless you happen to be a plant lover and, like me, you would want to make constant changes to the planting. The plants already set in their special holes will do fine, but how can you allow the gravel garden through the series of changes that are so essential for its development? A certain amount of extra planting will be possible, but every time that membrane is cut, the risk of weeds appearing through is increased. Thus, if your aim is merely to furnish a seldom-viewed corner with a few trouble-free shrubs, then membrane and gravel are fine. However, if you want to garden seriously, then lay gravel without the membrane, but be prepared to work harder to maintain it.

Here are details of some of the other likely problems with gravel, and some hints on how to solve them:

◆ **Incorporation with the soil.** Inevitably, over the years, gravel will tend to become blended with the soil beneath it. This will not hurt the plants, but will tend to make the top few inches of root space very free draining, which will be beneficial to arid-loving species, helping to prevent them from rotting off in wet winters. The rate at which the gravel disappears into the soil can be reduced if you are careful never to dig too deep, keeping hoe and rake set very shallow. When planting, scrape all the gravel carefully away before digging the hole, and remove any surplus soil, before replacing the gravel. Every few years, it may be necessary to top up your gravel garden with a thin layer of extra pebbles.

◆ **Soil spoiling the surface.** Frequently, soil is left on the surface after planting. This will wash through in heavy rain.

◆ **Excessive seeding.** Catch unwanted rashes of seedlings young. Merely moving the gravel about with your fingers could do the trick, when they first emerge, but if you leave them too long, expect a tougher problem.

◆ **Removal of gravel.** If you change your plans, and want to remove a gravel garden, do not expect to be able to recover everything down to the last stone. Once laid, gravel is difficult to collect up again. Simply scrape together what you can and be grateful that what is left will help to improve drainage.

Lawns and Grass

There are plenty of books devoted exclusively to lawn care, and it is well beyond the scope of this one to go into exhaustive detail about how to look after your grass. It may be helpful, however, to touch on the rudiments of lawn maintenance.

Routine maintenance is simple enough. Mow regularly, but never cut too closely, as this will increase the risk of moss in winter and will make the lawn more susceptible to drought damage in summer. I have always considered a rotary mower to be kinder to grass than a cylinder type, and unless you are a perfectionist, demanding cricket pitch or bowling green perfection, a rotary mower will cut grass neatly enough. Rotary mowers with rear rollers produce the better finish, with those sought-after stripes across the turf. Increase the intervals between mowing in autumn and stop altogether when the grass has stopped growing. If making a late cut, avoid mowing if frost is forecast. Also, mowing in wet weather is never a good idea.

It is only necessary to feed grass once – in early spring, as soon as the soil has warmed up and the grass is growing rapidly. Any moss or 'thatch' – dead grass stems and debris tangled among the turf – can be raked out, or removed with a mechanical scarifier during the spring, and any drainage problems can be put right in the autumn.

◆ **Lawn repairs.** Dips or bare patches that have appeared in the lawn can be repaired in early autumn, as soon as the ground has softened after rain. Dips should have turf removed, soil placed in the dip to compensate, and the turf then replaced. Bare areas can be re-turfed, but it is as easy to scrape the surface a little, and re-seed. Make sure no one walks over the re-seeded area and, if necessary, place a net over it to deter any seed-eating birds.

Areas of lawn that repeatedly wear can be reinforced with special material made out of shredded used tyres, or can have stepping stones set into the turf. If you go for the latter option, make sure the turf is slightly proud of the stone, to avoid any possible mower damage. Occasionally, the stepping stones may become overgrown by grass, and can have excess turf trimmed along their edges.

Lawn edges that have eroded are easy to repair by removing turf along the length of the edge, and reinstalling it with the clean cut outwards and the frayed edge laid against the lawn. Use a guide line or taut string, to make sure the edge is level and straight, and consider using an edging strengthener or laying a single line of paving between lawn and border. If the pavers are set a little lower than the turf, mowing along the sides of the lawn will be made very much easier, and plants in the border will be able to spill over.

OTHER LIVING SURFACES
Meadow Gardening

The days have gone, thankfully, when the only lawn acceptable in the eyes of a professional gardener was a faultless,

RIGHT *Use a membrane beneath your gravel if you are planning only to 'dot' small plants around your Alpine scree or gravel garden, but be prepared for harder work without a membrane if you require more plants.*

uniform, weed-free sward. Nowadays, it is not only acceptable for lawns to sport daisies, speedwell and other weeds, but in some areas it is actively encouraged. This liberalization makes lawn care easier, and more difficult at the same time. Removal of the task of weeding the grass makes things easier, but how many weeds are acceptable? If too many develop at the expense of the grass, parts of the lawn may become less hard-wearing, and could even result in bare patches. If fertilizer is used, however, the grass will grow more vigorously, and squeeze out the wild flowers. What to do? The answer is to make your decision as to which has priority – grass or flowers – and act accordingly. A feed with high nitrogen fertilizer, on very poor soils, may be necessary every few years to keep grass in the dominant position, but if you want a pure wildflower meadow, where broad-leaved plants rule in a background of mixed grasses, then never, ever feed, but rather let nature take its course.

As we saw on pages 72–4, grass is a wonderful medium for growing other plants. But where mowing is concerned, timing is crucial. Spring bulbs, summer meadow flowers, autumn displays and winter plants may all be grown in grass, but will all need a different approach. Here are some summarized guidelines:

◆ **Winter flowers.** Such as snowdrops, aconites, crocuses. Mow as normal, but do not make the first cut until the bulb leaves have withered. If you can allow their seed heads to ripen, so much the better. Expect this to happen in mid- to late spring, and for the first couple of cuts to look a little rough!

LEFT *Grass and gravel are considerably easier to maintain when planted or laid alone rather than with other materials mixed in. A simple garden floor with a centrepiece such as this one enables the gardener to spend more time tending the surrounding plants.*

◆ **Spring meadow.** If cut before seeding, cowslips, fritillaries and other spring flowers will diminish in numbers. The first cut may not, therefore, be possible until July. The resulting hay should be left to dry for a few days and then turned, so that the seeds can shed, before being raked off. Regular mowing can then ensue until winter, but keep the grass longish, to allow basal foliage of the broad-leaved plants to develop.

◆ **Summer meadow.** Treat as the spring meadow, but refrain from subsequent mowing so that the second flush of blooms can provide a display. You may wish to make a second cut in mid-autumn.

◆ **Autumn flowers.** As with the summer meadow, but make your last cut in late August, so that colchicums, autumn cyclamen and autumnal crocuses can bloom. There may be time for a quick cut in early winter.

Although meadow gardening has been practised for more than a century, there is still much to be learnt about how best to manage the grassland. In nature, the battle between grass and broadleaved plants is ceaseless. Grass, if unchecked, will drive out flowers on rich soils, whereas in poor conditions, especially where heavy grazing takes place, broad-leaved plants tend to dominate the grasses. The secret is to try to re-create a situation of poor fertility and therefore weak grass growth. In old-fashioned agriculture, the prettiest hay meadows were those where the farmer harvested his hay very late, after the plants had set seed, so in a garden it is best to cut the long grass back as late in summer as you can, and to allow the 'hay' to shed its seeds before raking off.

Other living floors can be made from camomile – see page 78 – a mixture of thymes, or almost any other low-growing, mat-forming plants.

Plant Care

Plants, if well selected and growing in ideal conditions, will virtually look after themselves. Most routine gardening jobs consist of checking that plants do not run short of nutrients or water. If your plant collection has been judiciously made, disease should seldom create major problems, and pests, apart from slugs and snails, are usually relatively easy to control. The underlying need, as with all gardening management, is to anticipate problems before they crop up.

Ninety percent of plant care lies in choosing the right plants in the first place. Your aim must be to find varieties that are resistant to disease, that will soldier on in an independent spirit, that will stand on their own feet without the need for extensive supports and that will bulk up or become well established with minimal effort. If your soil preparation has been sound, and the conditions are at least reasonably stable, planting should largely be a process of digging holes, popping in the plants, watering them and making sure their roots are firm, and then just standing back to watch them grow. Of course, there are certain plants – blue meconopsis, from the Himalayas, for example, or some of the terrestrial orchids – that are so special and gorgeous that you will ache to have them. And a handful of such plants will be well worth the extra bother. But if your rank and file planting is easily grown, easily maintained material, you will have more time to devote on this small selection of special beauties.

Planting. Some handy hints:

◆ **Space out the plants**, placing them exactly where you want them, before actually digging the holes and putting them in. This may take a while, since you will want to juggle them a little, but taking time over positioning them correctly at this stage will save time overall.

◆ **Always allow for expansion** – even when you do, you are bound to underestimate the extent to which the plants will grow.

◆ **Add a little bone meal** to the planting hole, especially when planting trees or shrubs.

◆ **Water thoroughly** at planting time, and again when the plants are in danger of drying out, throughout their first season. This is particularly important for trees and shrubs.

◆ **Contained plants** can be bought and planted at any time, but wherever possible, plan to do the bulk of your planting in autumn or early spring, preferably while the plants are still dormant. This will help them to get off to a good start.

Feeding

The tendency among most gardeners is to over-feed their plants. It is worth reminding ourselves that plants build themselves – not from nutrients in the ground, but from carbon dioxide in the air. The minerals that they need to do

RIGHT *One easy way to manage plants in your garden floor is to establish a sink garden like this one. A massed collection of sinks brings you all the benefits of container gardening with good area coverage.*

this come from the ground, of course, but are only required in minute quantities. If you ever worry about whether to give your plants a feed or not, spare a moment to consider some of our beautiful wild habitats. Who fertilizes the stunning mountain meadows of the Alps or the Rockies? No one. Who feeds the lush, wetland plants with their sumptuous flowers? No one. Artificial feeding is for artificial situations, and if you garden naturalistically, your plants will get by with minimal extra fertilizer.

A good general policy is to feed herbaceous perennials lightly in spring – I spread home-made compost over as many of my border plants as I can – and scatter general compound fertilizer (Growmore) at the rate of a single handful per two square metres – or thereabouts. It is very hit and miss. Trees and shrubs are never fed in my garden, except for roses, since these are cut back very hard, and produce a large number of flowers.

Container-grown plants must be fed, since they live in an artificial situation. Mine are fed every ten days with a proprietary liquid feed in the growing season. Frequently, I forget to feed; equally frequently, my plants forgive me by not noticing.

Routine Maintenance

Most plants benefit from a little tidying from time to time, involving removing faded flowers, or sometimes cutting exhausted flower stems right back to

encourage secondary growth. And even if such picking over does not stimulate production of new shoots, it will, at least, improve the appearance of your plants.

Thinning is important for self-seeding annuals and biennials. Remove enough seedlings to give the remainder the opportunity to reach their full potential. Although the more obviously weak plants should go, if colours are mixed, resist the temptation to save only the largest and most robust, since by doing so you could be sacrificing some of the more unusual colours.

Almost all perennials benefit from occasional dividing. The exceptions are those with deep tap roots, and those, such as paeonies and hellebores, which develop relatively slowly. Lift the plants in autumn or spring, and divide ruthlessly into small sections, each with its own roots and a couple of shoots, and replant into ground that has been prepared by digging over and dressed with rotted manure or a little compost. Perennials that have become established in paving cracks, or at wall footings, would be difficult to replant and are better left alone.

Pruning and Training

Pruning and training is only necessary with certain plants, either to keep them to a desired size and shape, or, as with roses, to stimulate production of bloom. Hedges need clipping, of course, but the great majority – including box, yew, holly, beech, hornbeam and conifers – will get by perfectly well with a single annual cut. This is best carried out in late summer when the year's growth is more or less complete. Privet, Elaeagnus and *Lonicera nitida* may need more than one cut.

LEFT *Some plants will benefit from a little judicious deadheading, pruning or general thinning. But do not overdo it. Remember that many garden plants manage perfectly well in the wild without any attention at all.*

they have a free run in open ground and certain minerals will begin to run short. During the first part of the growing season, use a high-nitrogen feed to foster rapid growth. As soon as flowering begins, or when the flowering season is getting close, change your regime to a high-potassium feed. Alternatives to liquid feed include slow release pills or pellets, fertilizer tablets and fertilizer sticks. These are easier, but regular feeding with liquid fertilizer gives you more control. If the plants are growing too proud and lush, or look hungry, you can adjust your feeding accordingly.

Trouble Shooting – Pests and Diseases

In a well managed, balanced garden, diseases and pests should seldom cause serious problems. They will be there – they are everywhere! – but they are unlikely to destroy plants, or to threaten the display. But in certain years, you might experience problems, and if you grow disease-prone plants you will need to follow a disease control programme. Roses, Michaelmas daisies, delphiniums and bergamot are all examples of plants that tend to suffer. Preventative sprays will help to keep them clean, but a better way is to grow only disease-resistant forms.

As for pests, if you have a wildlife-friendly garden with a good balance of plants, pest problems will be less serious than they would be in a manicured, but sterile plot. Encouraging predators of sap-sucking creatures will help enormously. Ladybirds, hover flies, lacewings, small song birds and ground beetles will all help in your war efforts against undesirable pests. Hedgehogs and amphibians are unsurpassable for gobbling up slugs and snails, and should also be made welcome. Hints on how to harbour wildlife follow.

Climbers and wall plants used to decorate the vertical surfaces surrounding your new garden floor will need a certain amount of tying in during the growing season, but may require a more fundamental overhaul once a year, during the dormant period. Roses, for example, can be completely removed from their supports, to make pruning and training easier. The old wood is removed, but younger stems – especially those that have grown from a bud during the current season – should be retained and tied in, preferably flexed towards the horizontal, to stimulate better flowering. A fan shape formation enables optimum surface coverage.

Weak-stemmed climbers, such as clematis, can be encouraged to grow through stronger 'wall plants' to make an effective plant association. Some can be trained to grow out and over the garden floor as well as upwards. Take care with your selection, however, since those that flower before the longest day should not be winter-pruned, as all the flowers are borne on the previous season's growth. Better to select later blooming kinds, such as the hybrids of *C. viticella* which come in a rich colour range and can be cut to ground level, if necessary, every winter.

When blends of climbers are grown, watch carefully for invasive species which may overwhelm less vigorous varieties. In time, a congested mass of mixed climbers could develop, but if these are pruned hard most will regenerate with speed, enabling you to regain control, but returning to a full display quickly.

Special Care for Containers

All containerized plants need feeding during the growing season. However well chosen your containers may be, roots are bound to be more restricted than when

Wildlife Considerations

In a rapidly urbanizing world, and with intensive agriculture dominating the countryside, gardens are becoming increasingly important as havens for wildlife. Endangered species and creatures of great rarity are constantly in the news, but there is also a huge retinue of species which were recently abundant but which are now suffering population crashes. If you are concerned about this, and would like to have some influence in trying to prevent population decline – or if you just like the idea of having wild things at large in your garden – it is worth trying to do your growing in a wildlife-friendly way. Even if you do not care especially about wild species, there are still a number of gardening practices you can adopt which will not only improve the natural habitat, but will actually make your garden look better.

The biggest enemy of wildlife is the obsessively tidy gardener. Strimming right up to the edges of trees, removing every trace of long grass, preventing undergrowth from developing among shrubs and clearing away every scrap of natural debris, all remove valuable habitat for the insects and other creatures which are not only beneficial, but which provide a valuable food source for birds.

If you can resist the temptation to cut back perennials in the autumn, leaving their dying stems until late winter or early spring, the benefits to wildlife are substantial and, on balance, the practice is better for perennials too, especially those that benefit from a little winter protection. Many look particularly attractive in winter anyway – Centaurea seed heads, or dead sedums look ravishing when dusted with snow or hoar

LEFT *These plants are beautifully tended and manicured, tying in with the pristine white gravel around them. But sometimes it is kinder to the environment – and particularly wildlife – to let things go a little.*

frost – and if they still carry seed, you may be treated to the sight of goldfinches feeding in the winter sunlight.

Propagating and Replacing Plants

If you want to keep your plant population healthy, it will be necessary to do a little propagating. This does not mean that you have to go into the nursery business – indeed, you can purchase all your replacements, if you prefer. However, since propagation is one of the most enjoyable aspects of gardening as a hobby, it seems pointless to develop the perfect garden design and planting scheme if you are planning to forego one of gardening's great pleasures! Here are a few categories of propagation techniques that will enable you to obtain plants for free every year.

◆ **Cuttings.** Most of the tender summer material grown in gardens as annuals are technically perennial and can be grown year after year. Petunias, lobelias, pelargoniums, nasturtiums, impatiens and begonias are but a few examples and can all be rooted very easily from cuttings. The month that follows the summer solstice is the optimum period for this, partly because it gives the plants time to root and mature before winter sets in, and partly because a plant's hormone system is such that rooting is quicker and easier at that time of year. Soft cuttings, as these summer ones are called, should not be more than 3–6cm (1–2in) long, should have their lower leaves removed, their stems cut across a leaf joint (node) and should be inserted into a sharp-draining compost in a small pot. If you have a propagator, set the cutting into it, with a bottom temperature of around 21°C (68°F). If you don't have a propagator, get one!

◆ **Seed.** It is easier to raise plants from seed than most novice gardeners think. Many can be directly sown into seedbeds in open ground. Hardy perennials will

germinate readily if sown in free-draining compost in seed pans which are placed in a coldframe, or a part of the garden which is protected from extremes of temperature. Seed which needs bottom heat and protection from frost is a little more challenging, especially if you do not possess a greenhouse, but is still a fine way to produce plants in large numbers. Every seed has its own preferred set of conditions for germination – some must be frozen and thawed, some need light, others must be kept in the dark – so it is worth studying instructions on the seed packet, or, with seed you have collected yourself, to find out as much as possible about the seeds' needs. Trial and error will reward you with considerable seed raising skill.

◆ **Division.** This is the ideal way not only to multiply herbaceous perennials but also certain suckering shrubs. Most perennials actually require division, in order to remain young and vigorous. The secret for success is to be utterly ruthless in your dividing, splitting the plant down to individual shoots.

◆ **Layering.** The solution to propagating plants that are reluctant to root from cuttings and will not come true from seed. Rhododendrons are candidates for layering, as are such climbing plants as honeysuckles and clematis. The technique is to select a branch that grows close to the ground, make an oblique cut, halfway through the stem, and wedge the wound open with a matchstick or a tuft of moss. Then submerge that point in the stem into the soil, and anchor it down with a rock or wire peg. The new plant may take two years to fully develop, but develop it will.

Crisis Management with Planting

With planting, nothing is truly permanent. If builders happen to wreck a border along the house, or at the edges of a terrace, you can effect first aid by removing victims and arranging containers or planting containerized plants. Ugly gaps may well appear in a border designed for an early summer climax, but are easy to fill with tender material that has been brought on elsewhere. The current trend for growing substantial tropical plants – cannas,

bananas, solanums and so on – in cold regions has helped to ensure glorious displays until the first frost. And such displays can be added to steadily, through the season, right up to the last month of summer.

Your own mistakes – and there will be many – are also easy to rectify. No one gets it right first, or even second and third times. Indeed, one of the most enjoyable aspects of gardening is to have the time and the inclination to tinker about with your planting schemes, gradually evolving beauty throughout the garden, year on year.

Finally, here are my **Ten Golden Rules** for successful planting and plant maintenance:
1. **Only grow plants that you like.**
2. **Only grow plants that like your garden's conditions.**
3. **Only grow plants that will live happily together.**
4. **Plants must fit their surroundings.**
5. **No plant should be allowed to threaten its neighbour.**
6. **All plants should be easy to grow, or, if not, should pay off extra effort with a huge reward.**
7. **All plants must pay their rent. Only those which make a good contribution to your garden should be grown.**
8. **The plant must be the best example of its kind – go for the finest varieties.**
9. **All plants should be able to thrive without needing disease control.**
10. **Plants should carry more than one asset – for example, autumn foliage, spring flowers, winter twigs, good seedheads.**

And the greatest of these is the first, namely, grow what you like!

ABOVE *Whatever you decide to do to improve your garden floor, remember that it will always be among the most noticeable of the features in your garden. Choose your materials carefully and make it look its best.*

Glossary

Some of the projects in this book involve building work rather than pure gardening skills – particularly those garden floors that require hard landscaping – so a number of technical terms and names of tools and materials are used that might be unfamiliar to some readers. This glossary provides a basic explanation of these and other terms.

Algae Diverse group of mainly aquatic plants. Blanket weed in ponds and seaweed are examples.

Boardwalk A pathway of raised decking, usually constructed over uneven ground.

Brickbats Pieces of hardcore, usually bits of old brick.

Brick bonding The means by which a brick construction is given its strength. More than merely a pattern in the brickwork, it ensures that the whole fabric, be it wall or paving, is held together firmly without any 'seams', which would create weakness.

Carboniferous Limestone which is carbon bearing – i.e. coal bearing.

Forest bark By-product of the forestry industry, where harvested trees are stripped of their bark which is then pulverized and packaged for use as mulch or compost.

Frost pocket Low-lying area of land where cold air can accumulate on cold nights, resulting in ground temperatures which are lower than those of higher surroundings. If these dip below freezing point, localized frost occurs.

Grouting The filling of spaces between tiles or paving with mortar or special plaster material to create a perfect finish.

Growmore Not a brand name, but a British-approved compound artificial fertilizer.

Hoggin A mixture of sand and gravel which tends to set solid when laid down and rolled.

Maquis The rocky, arid terrain, furnished with low-growing, spiky shrubs, that borders most of the Mediterranean shores.

Mulch A layer of bulky material laid over the soil surface to reduce evaporation rate from the ground and to help to suppress weed development.

Oölitic limestone Literally means egg bearing. A kind of limestone composed of small rounded beads (ooliths) which resemble fish roe.

Parterre Specially levelled or terraced area of a garden divided up with formal patterns of beds and pathways.

pH Literally, the negative decimal logarithm of hydrogen ion concentration in moles per litre. In practice, it is a measure of acidity or alkalinity.

Polypropylene Tough artificial plastic, usually used by gardeners in woven form as a weed-proof membrane or layer through which water can freely drain.

Polyurethane Plastic varnish material for coating surfaces outdoors and in, to protect from moisture and wear.

Potash Chemical element essential for both plant and animal life. Occurs naturally in soil, and in most organic material.

Scalpings Small chips and shavings of stone, often used in foundations on top of, or as an alternative to, hardcore.

Scree The loose rock and pebble debris which forms at the base of cliffs or steep rock slopes, usually as a result of frost erosion. In a garden, the term 'scree' refers to a kind of gravel culture which features plants that might occur in natural screes.

Screed Piece of wood or plank for levelling unset concrete.

Shaling The tendency of rock, and also terracotta, to perish when exposed to weathering, by forming fragile layers which gradually come apart.

Shuttering The name given to the wooden channels constructed for directing concrete when it is poured.

Sward The surface or turf of a lawn or a green area.

Thatch (in lawns) Dead or moribund grassy material – stems and leaves – which accumulates at the bases of the grass plants in a lawn.

Vista Any long, narrow view, perhaps bordered by trees, or by high walls.

Vista 'stop' An object designed to attract attention when placed at the end of a vista.

Yin and yang The two constructing principles of the universe, as viewed by Chinese philosophers. Yang represents the active, male principle – as seen in jagged, standing rocks or tumbling waters – whereas Yin is passive and female, seen in still waters and gently rounded rocks.

Suppliers & Useful Addresses

Most of the tools, materials and plants used in the projects at the heart of this book are widely available from garden centres, DIY superstores, builder's yards, salvage centres and hardware stores. If you have difficulty tracking down a particular material or tool, ask your local garden centre for advice. Here are the names and addresses of some leading suppliers.

UNITED KINGDOM

Alpine Garden Society
AGS Centre, Pershore, Worcs WR10 3JP
Tel: 01386 554790
Advice about alpine gardens and plants.

B&Q plc
Portswood House, 1 Hampshire Corporate Park, Chandlers Ford, Hants SO53 3YX Tel: 01703 256256
General building tools and materials.

Bridgemere Garden World
Nantwich, Cheshire CW5 7QB
Tel: 01270 521100
Plants and gardening equipment.

Hardy Plant Society
Little Orchard, Great Comberton, Pershore, Worcs WR10 3DP
Tel: 01386 710317
Advice on hardy plants.

Hillier Nurseries Ltd
Ampfield House, Romsey, Hants SO51 9PA Tel: 01794 368733
Plants and gardening equipment.

Jewson Ltd
Sutherland House, Matlock Road, Foleshill, Coventry CV1 4JQ
Tel: 01203 669100
General building tools and materials.

Notcutts Garden Centres
Woodbridge, Suffolk IP12 4AF
Tel: 01394 445400
Plants and gardening equipment.

Royal Horticultural Society (RHS)
80 Vincent Square, London SW1P 2PE
Tel: 0171 834 4333
General gardening advice and information.

Wyevale Nurseries
Kings Acre, Hereford HR4 7AY
Tel: 01432 352255
Plants and general gardening equipment.

SOUTH AFRICA

Consult your telephone directory for your local branch of **Mica Hardware** or **Federated Timbers**.

Dunrobin Garden Pavilion
Old Main Road, Bothas Hill, Durban
Tel: (031) 777 1855

Garden World
Muldersdrif Road, Honeydew, Johannesburg
Tel: (011) 957 2046

Radermachers Garden & Home Centre
Kraaibosch, National Road, George
Tel: (044) 889 0075/6

Safari Garden Centre
Lynwood Road, Pretoria
Tel: (012) 807 0009

Showgrounds Nursery
Showgrounds, Currie Avenue, Bloemfontein
Tel: (051) 447 5523

Starke Ayres (Pty) Ltd
Liesbeek Road, Rosebank, Cape Town
Tel: (021) 685 4120

AUSTRALIA

BBC Hardware
Building A, Cnr Chester & Cambridge Streets, Epping, NSW 2121
Tel: (02) 8876 0898

Cascade Nurseries Pty Ltd
Lot 2, McAllister Road, Monbulk 3793
Tel: (039) 756 7557

Flower Power Stores
Head Office, 124 Newbridge Road, Moorebank, NSW 2170
Tel: (02) 9601 4555

Garden King Products Pty Ltd
PO Box 6130, Parramatta, Bc NSW 2150
Tel: (02) 9871 3700

Schroder Landscapes
50 Station Street, Belgrave, Vic 3160
Tel: (03) 9752 5127

NEW ZEALAND

Hammer Hardware
Stores nationwide
Head Office Tel: (09) 443 0025

Kings Plant Barn Ltd
Glenfield, Howick, Remuera and St Lukes Auckland
Tel: (09) 410 9726

Mitre 10
Stores nationwide
Head Office Tel: (09) 443 9900

Palmers Gardenworld
Stores nationwide
Head Office Tel: (09) 443 9910

Placemakers
Stores nationwide
Head Office Tel: (09) 525 5100

Index

This index chiefly comprises the tools and materials you will need to complete the projects that make up the backbone of the book. For ease of reference, the projects are listed both under their own names and under the general heading 'Projects'. In the same way, key materials are listed twice, in their own names and under a generic heading.

Acknowledgements

The author and publishers would like to thank the many people who contributed to the making of this book. Alan Gray, Maurice Green, Paul Reed, Graham Robeson and Ian Sidaway all deserve special mention for kindly allowing Laura Wickenden and Focus Publishing into their gardens to take photographs specially for the book. Detailed photographic credits are given below.

Focus Publishing

pp17 (garden of Ian Sidaway); 38; 39; 44; 45; 49; 50; 58; 62; 66; 67; 68; 71 (garden of Ian Sidaway); 72; 73; 76; 77; 104–5; 122.

The Garden Picture Library

pp 12 (Steven Wooster); 19 (Eric Crichton); 25; 26 (Henk Dijkman); 30 (Howard Rice); 31 (Henk Dijkman); 47 (Ron Sutherland); 52 (Ron Sutherland); 79 (Marijke Heuff); 82; 88–9 (Juliette Wade); 98 (Juliet Greene); 108–9 (Brian Carter; 116–17 (Eric Crichton); 119 (Mel Watson).

Jerry Harpur

pp 10–11; 13; 14; 15; 18; 20–21 (garden of Beth Chatto); 22; 28; 29 (Cabbages & Kings); 32–3; 34; 35; 51; 61; 68–9 (garden of Patrick Miller); 83 (Barnsley House); 97 (designer: Dan Pearson); 99.

Marcus Harpur

pp 2; 41; 63; 80.

Andrew Lawson

pp 43; 52–3; 85.

Clive Nichols

pp 65 (design by David Stevens and Julian Dowle); 102–3 (Andrew and Carla Newell).

Derek St Romaine

pp 8; 36–7; 70; 120–21.

Laura Wickenden

pp 1; 6 (garden of Alan Gray and Graham Robeson, East Ruston Old Vicarage Garden); 23 (garden of Alan Gray and Graham Robeson); 48 (garden of Alan Gray and Graham Robeson); 55 (garden of Alan Gray and Graham Robeson); 57 (garden of Paul Reed); 59 (garden of Maurice Green); 75 (garden of Alan Gray and Graham Robeson); 81 (garden of Alan Gray and Graham Robeson); 86–7 (garden of Maurice Green); 90 (garden of Alan Gray and Graham Robeson); 91 (garden of Maurice Green); 93 (garden of Alan Gray and Graham Robeson); 95–5 (garden of Alan Gray and Graham Robeson); 101; 106 (garden of Alan Gray and Graham Robeson); 110–11 (garden of Paul Reed); 113; 114–15 (garden of Alan Gray and Graham Robeson); 118 (garden of Paul Reed; model Mrs Reed); 127.

Jacket photographs by Focus Publishing (back and spine detail); Garden Picture Library/Marijke Heuff (bottom right); Jerry Harpur (top left; bottom left); Derek St Romaine (top right).